Dazzling
Darkness

For
John & Gordon, doctors extraordinaire,
who have kept me alive and mostly flourishing
and most particularly
my family
for their transforming love.

Dazzling Darkness

Gender, Sexuality, Illness & God

Rachel Mann

wild goose
publications

www.**ionabooks**.com

First published 2012, reprinted 2013, 2017

Wild Goose Publications
21 Carlton Court, Glasgow G5 9JP, UK
www.ionabooks.com
Wild Goose Publications is the publishing division of the Iona Community.
Scottish Charity No. SC003794. Limited Company Reg. No. SC096243.

ISBN 978-1-84952-241-0

The publishers gratefully acknowledge the support of the Drummond Trust,
3 Pitt Terrace, Stirling FK8 2EY in producing this book.

Cover image © Lauren Shulz for Nanamee

A catalogue record for this book is available from the British Library.

Overseas distribution:
Australia: Willow Connection Pty Ltd, Unit 4A, 3-9 Kenneth Road,
Manly Vale, NSW 2093
New Zealand: Pleroma, Higginson Street, Otane 4170, Central Hawkes Bay
Canada: Novalis/Bayard Publishing & Distribution, 10 Lower Spadina Ave.,
Suite 400, Toronto, Ontario M5V 2Z2

Printed by Bell & Bain, Thornliebank, Glasgow

Contents

*And in the dark
as we slept
the world
was made flesh.*

Eavan Boland, 'Hymn'

Foreword

'The desert dreams'

Nothing in the affairs of humankind is by its very nature as ambiguous as religious faith. And no doubt every religious person should ask: 'Where, exactly, does my faith come from?'

Is it a mere outgrowth of 'herd morality'? In other words, essentially a matter of belonging-together with other people more or less like myself, in mutual self-congratulation and perhaps mistrust of the wider world. Is this, secretly, what has shaped my mental picture of God?

Well, here's the story of someone whose faith quite clearly doesn't come from *that* source! Rachel is someone to whom not much else that's human is alien, but where's the *herd* that she could belong to? It certainly isn't to be found within the Church of England, where she's ended up. Of course, there *are* a number of different herds around within the Church. But none that could include someone like her.

Sceptics often assume that religious faith springs from a desire to be comforted: at bottom, mere self-pity, a yearning for heavenly sanction and for consolatory reassurance from on high. Rachel's is, amongst other things, a tale of many misfortunes. But observe: it's told here without the slightest trace of such self-pity. Superficial readers may be incredulous of this – and project onto the text the self-pity *they'd* be tempted to feel in her situation. Indeed, it's virtually impossible for a writer of autobiography to preclude such misreading. However, let me testify: I know Rachel – and, really, I've seldom met anyone who, so far as I can tell, is less motivated by self-pity than she is.

It seems to me that what she represents is a whole other species of religious faith. Namely, something like *an option for all-transformative ultimate acceptance*. So far as I understand it, her faith seems to be a sheer celebration of life, come what may. I guess it takes some courage to make public a story like the one that follows, risking the world's crass prurience and confronting it. Indeed, Rachel's faith is quite clearly bound up with the reckless moral courage of a natural dissident. Yet, this is dissent unspoilt by bitterness. Rather, it's nothing other than a principled recognition of the very clearest-eyed honesty – precisely, as a sacred ideal. Her telling of her story is theologically interesting, above all because of the vivid way it illustrates *that* species of faith.

In short, here's someone who appears to embody all the 'Dionysian' virtues so entertainingly, and so thought-provokingly, celebrated by Friedrich Nietzsche and his many followers to this day. Only minus the typical Nietzschean vice of intellectual conceit, the one *truly* God-less element in their doctrine. She's quite free of that – as is evidenced by her also being such a good priest.

For my part, I've actually only ever known Rachel as a very capable, sane and level-headed Anglican parish priest, much loved (I sense) by her parishioners, both at St Matthew's Stretford and St Nicholas Burnage. Prejudice whispers to me that one wouldn't *expect* a person with a back-story like hers to be as effortlessly at ease with people, in general, as she is. But it helps that she has so much laughter within her. Here, indeed, is a priest who quite plainly can see the funny side of the divine comedy, in its defiant, final aspiration to encompass all tragedy.

And this is a woman who can write, too. She's our Cathedral poet. A little while ago, for instance, we published the following poem of hers in our *Manchester Cathedral News*:

Kenosis

'Let this avail, just, dreadful, mighty God
This not all be in vain', 'St Simeon Stylites', Tennyson

Who would not
stretch an arm up
above their head
pushing tiptoe high –
precarious as a dancing girl –
reaching for the belly of a cloud?

Who would not
rip their tongue
tear open their lips to try
hawk song? Locust talk?

I have tried only to understand
the voice which insists we must
go up to go further in.

Up here all things fall away.
The flower blooms, the flower dies.

The desert dreams.

'We must / go up to go further in ...' I take 'up' to mean flying up
– hawk-like or even locust-like – beyond the earthbound, original
banality of a life confined to mere prevailing moral norms. 'Who
would not' reach for the sacred mystery hidden in 'the belly of a
cloud' – if only they knew how? *Most of us would not!* We're just
too afraid of the 'rip' and 'tear' liable to be involved in the
'stretching up'; whether becoming proud 'hawk', or self-depre-
cating 'locust'. But look – here, by contrast, is the story of a
'dancing girl' who 'would'.

What else, indeed, is the basic purpose of God's primordial *kenosis*, or self-emptying in the Incarnation, if not to invite a similar response from us: our being emptied of the all too easy, earthbound identities that the world confers on us from birth? No one is exempt from this. Here, though, is someone who has experienced that universal calling, the calling to remake herself, in pretty well the most fiercely challenging form possible.

And look how she has seized the opportunity!

Andrew Shanks
Manchester Cathedral
Good Friday 2012

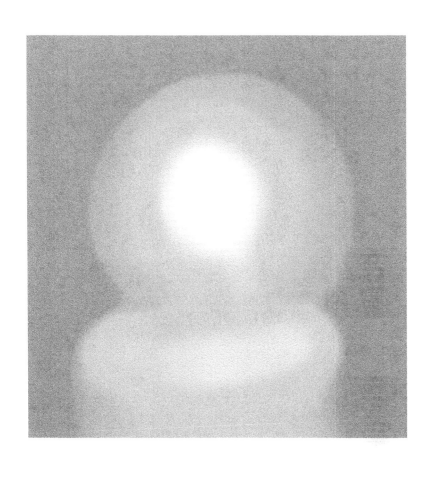

Introduction

Perhaps there was a time when I could have told a hundred stories about myself. Now I realise I only have one that matters. I've spent half my life wishing it were otherwise; wishing that my story would be glamorous, heroic, admirable or, indeed, simple. But that is not what I have to offer. The only story I have is a confession.

In many ways I am not proud of what I have to tell. For this confession – even if it is the story of an honest wrestling with my longings for wholeness, for the Divine and self-knowledge – is really the story of failure and loss. And of the hope that remains in the midst of them. It is a story, in some respects, then, about what is conventionally seen as 'darkness'. And yet I have discovered that though darkness is normally seen as negative, it is as much a positive place as anything else. It is a place, I believe, inhabited by the Living God – what I want to call the Dark God or the Hidden God. This is the God that many of us, because we try to make our lives safe and comfortable, are too afraid to meet. And so this is an account of my wanderings in the company of the Dark or Hidden God: the God who comes to us beyond our comfortable categories; who meets us in the darkness; who is most alive in those things we commonly associate with the Dark – failure, loss and brokenness. This is the God who will not be used and made to serve our ends and who therefore is the Living God. For as Meister Eckhart puts it, 'To use God is to kill him.'

There is, I shall suggest, something profoundly troubling about this God – for this is the kind of God whose grace can come as harshly and violently as the angel who wrestles with Jacob; this is the God whose grace threatens to gouge out an eye. And so this is not the God of easy consolation, but because of that she has the wondrous benefit of actually being real.

This is a book, then, about one unavoidable thing: the many faces of death. The focal point of this meditation on forms of dying is the loss of self and, ultimately, its recovery. And so, if it is a book about death, it is inevitably also a book about birth and new life. I hope that doesn't strike you as too gnomic: the simple fact is that death is intimately connected with birth and rebirth. As TS Eliot succinctly notes, 'In my end is my beginning.'

It is also a story of self-indulgence, self-deception, of wild experimentation, of drugs and rock 'n' roll, and of what might be said to pass for 'redemption' in times when words like faith and commitment are more likely to produce bewilderment and fear than enthusiasm. As such I hope that in the midst of the serious hand-wringing, it might be quite a lot of fun – for there is a lot of vicarious pleasure to be had in other people's rather tragi-comic and picaresque adventures. If this book could aspire to be one thing it would be a kind of 'Pilgrim's Progress' with all the tasty and dodgy bits left in.

But, at its heart, this is a story about intangible and, I want to argue, important things: it's about becoming who one is called to be. And its conclusion – in common with the likes of Merton, Ignatius of Loyola and spiritual explorers of all traditions – is that finally we are simply called to be ourselves. The only – and somewhat frustrating – problem is that, for us as humans, to be our true selves is such a tricky business. Thomas Merton[1] suggests that each of us can give no greater glory to God than being ourselves – our true selves. So it is for all creation: a tree gives glory to God by being a tree. But for the tree that's not a difficult thing

---

[1] Thomas Merton, *Seeds of Contemplation* (London: Burns & Oates 1962), Chapter 2.

to do – it cannot be other than its essential 'tree-ness'. For humans, on the other hand, it's terribly complicated. We have so many possibilities and paths before us. We carry the splinter of brokenness within us. And so the only way any of us can know and be truly ourselves is to know ourselves in God. For only God sees the picture clearly. Only God holds me in my completeness. A journey into self, then, is a journey into God.

There is a big part of me that knows the world doesn't really need another 'warts and all, redemption-based' spirituality book. But I have always been aware that at some point I would need to make some sort of effort at confession. In the end, I've been unable to resist setting it down, hoping that I can do it as honestly and accurately as possible. My confession, for what it's worth, is precisely about the 'paradox' or mystery of the self we have to lose and the self we have to find. This confession wrestles again and again with Jesus' most profound, troubling and frustrating statement: 'Those who seek to save their lives will lose it, but those who lose their life for my sake will save it.' I can think of no simpler and no more challenging calling than that to be oneself.

My own adventures – involving bouts of wild living, endless self-indulgence, a sex change, questions about my sexuality, and nasty, nasty chronic illness – have been nothing more or less than an adventure in becoming more myself in the wholeness that is God. It has been, and is, an adventure into places of both joy and considerable pain. It is a journey down into being – into being me by being in God. It is a mystery of connection – the more I know God, the more I know me and the more I know me, the more I know God.

It is also a journey into a kind of terror, which has entailed discovering that somehow in my acknowledged and real woundedness, in my messy brokenness, in the broken middle I inhabit, I am most me. It is into this place that Christ comes, the Christ whose wounds never heal, though she be risen; the Christ – the God – who holds the wound of love within her very being. For, so often, it is our very woundedness, our vulnerability, which feeds and heals us.

However, if this book is a kind of confession and an exploration of what it means to be the bearer of the image of God, then it is also a work of theology. That is to say, one of the seams running through this book, sometimes near the surface, sometimes submerged, is a question: in what sense are people like me (queer people) agents of grace and gifts to the church and beyond? For I sense that we are. And I hope that this intuition isn't merely an easy kind of self-justification. It is in order to avoid that pitfall that there is theology in this book. At least some attempt at creative and imaginative rigour will be offered. But there is need for a health warning here: this is not a work of systematic, academic theology. I have neither the brain nor the inclination for that project. Others have pursued and will pursue that path. This is a book that reaches for sense and a certain degree of precision, but seeks to do so in terms that are more poetic than academic. I am conscious that this approach runs the risk of being inconsistent, elliptical and perhaps even contradictory. I try for some measure of consistency, but if I fail I ask your indulgence. Trying to produce theology through the prism of a life rather than in the realms of pure ideas will always be messy.

Ultimately, this is the story of a divided self seeking to live more or less at peace with herself. It comes as no surprise to me, then, that at a theological level there is also a conceptual 'division' in dynamic tension. That division is between an apophatic and a kataphatic way to God.[2] So much of what I want to say here comes down to the idea that we cannot quite say who God is and as such

---

[2] While I wish to keep technical terms to a minimum, this distinction is a useful one, representing two ways of knowing God. The Apophatic or Negative Way (implying no moral judgement) suggests that God, in her deepest being, is unknowable and can only be known by what she is not. The Kataphatic or Positive Way suggests that humans can know God positively – that we can outline attributes and positive characteristics. This distinction is one of the key tensions in Christian theology and plays out dynamically in what I have to say.

we must ultimately be left in silence in her presence. And yet, again and again, in my life and in my theological reflection I feel invited by God to be expansive, to multiply the ways in which we speak of her. And if, ultimately, one must be silent before God in order to let her be God, I remain convinced that one must be unafraid to play wild language-games with her too. For perhaps it is only in the creative dynamic between Word and Waiting that we may hope to be our true selves.

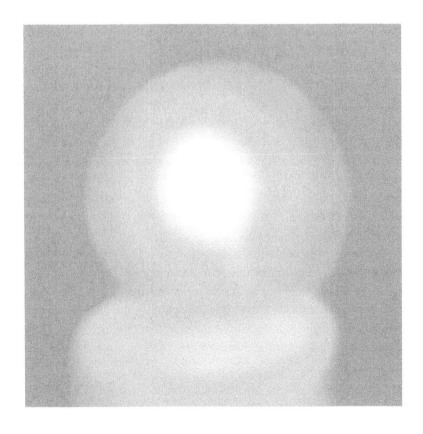

Prologue

A Tonka Toy Christmas[3]

I don't usually remember individual childhood Christmases. Like overused plasticine, all the distinctive colours blend into one mud brown. And in most respects Christmas day 1975 was not, by my family's 1970s' experience, a particularly unusual one. We were still very poor, a largish family cramped into a three bedroom semi-detached house, huddling around one coal fire for warmth during the day, we children getting lost in the deep polyester caverns of our sleeping bags at night. And yet this 'Tonka toy Christmas' glows yellow and black, roars like a 50-ton truck. It defines my childhood. Its importance lies in the iconic nature of the indestructible Tonka truck that I was given and adored. It was moulded plastic, but hard as nails. Its unbreakable shiny newness revealed, to a five year old, one of the faces of God. I straddled its black driver's cab and trundled off down the hall to the soundtrack of my own satisfyingly throaty chug.

This was, for me, the ultimate boy toy – more macho than Action Man's scar, bolder than Evel Knievel, better able to come back for more punishment than the Six Million Dollar Man. And the fact that I had one at five has rebounded, like a ball in a pinball machine, through my Christmases and my life ever since. For although one might argue that nothing could be more appropriate

---

[3] A version of this chapter can also be found in Slee & Miles, ed, *Doing December Differently* (Glasgow: Wild Goose Publications 2006).

for a five-year-old working-class boy than a yellow dumper truck, there was one problem: this five-year-old boy wanted, at a profound but hardly articulated level, to be a girl. But, even as a five year old, I was desperate for no one to glimpse – even catch a peek through my closed-fingered defences – this truth about me. No one must know. Ever.

And so the ultimate boy toy was the perfect present. That Tonka toy Christmas, I see now, symbolised and anticipated my life for the next 16 years. For, as I grew up and became ever more aware of my gender dysphoria, the more I sought to conceal it. How better, especially at Christmas, than to behave in ways that signify 'boy' and 'masculinity'? Even now, many years on from my gender change, I still work through the implications of the commitments I made at the age of five and it is Christmas that provides the focus for this. For not only is it when I typically spend an extended period with my immediate family, but it is also a time of intense family sharing and scrutiny.

Being a transsexual child is, by its very nature, uncomfortable, especially in a claustrophobic village where granny is twitching the curtains every five minutes to check you're behaving correctly. This was especially true in an age when the only press about 'sex changes' was confined to tabloid sensationalism. But discomfort doesn't prevent a small child from living, from trying to make the best of things. The ache of discomfort, of dysphoria, was simply that: an ache. And I became superb at disguise, pretending to be a perfectly ordinary boy and teenager. Sometimes, and typically at Christmas, that ache coalesced with other factors – choosing what presents to have, family expectations – into a painful knotty blockage. A cyst. The cyst grew fat and bloated and harder to disguise. I tried to ignore it. My teenage years not only were marked with the usual adolescent malaise of confusion and body discomfort experienced by almost everyone, but were attended by horror at what my body was becoming and an inability to talk about this to anyone.

Christmas 1990 was the logical, painful culmination of the

Tonka toy Christmas fifteen years before. For in 1975 I'd committed myself to being a 'normal little boy'; the Tonka toy was the sacramental sealing of my commitment. That commitment had just enough energy to last fifteen years. In 1990, in a state of depression, as I lay awake in bed in the early hours of Christmas day, I tried to renew the covenant, this time in the form of a prayer – a prayer to myself, to whatever God I believed in, to the God of hopeless causes. I couldn't stand the thought of being true to myself and I was desperate to avoid hurting my parents. I would, then, be heroic: I would embrace this hairy, muscly creature I'd grown into and live as a happy man – at least until such a time as everyone I might hurt by changing sex had died off. My 20-year-old self was superb at making grand gestures. This final gesture had momentum enough to keep me in public denial for another two years. At the end of that time I could no longer avoid the truth. The grand gesture collapsed. My family/friends and I began to talk, really talk. I dropped the little boy hands from my eyes and looked out, allowing myself to be looked upon, really looked upon, for the first time. I began the difficult and remarkable journey of changing sex.

Much of my early life was a process of being silenced – partly through conscious self-silencing, partly through the absorption of family, social and cultural mores. I could find no language in which to speak through taboos about gender identity. So I settled into silence. Silence – and breaking out of it – has been a key trope of my life. It is intriguing that so much personal silence has coalesced around my experience of Christmas. Perhaps inevitably, as someone who is both a priest and a theologian, I have wanted to interrogate the Nativity narratives in an attempt to locate myself within them. 'Who,' I've wanted to ask, 'represents the silenced in these narratives? Who represents the likes of me?' The answers to this question provide some of the theological sense I can find in Christmas from a transgendered perspective. Part of me is happy simply to ask the question and allow it to resonate; part of me wants to shake it like a Christmas tree, hoping that hidden treasure and presents will fall out.

If my Christmases (and my broader life) have typically been characterised by silence, how does God speak into that? When I read the gospels I am immediately struck by the fact that two of them – Mark and John – basically lack Christmas narratives. This is, no doubt, for all sorts of reasons, but I find this absence *as absence* both striking and strangely encouraging; it is as if Jesus himself has lost his nativity, his origins, his childhood. It has been silenced because it has not been included. Or, to come at it another way, the wholeness of Jesus is not compromised because a childhood or a birth narrative has not been included. Jesus is whole – even as much of his story is silenced.

Even in Matthew and Luke – which have Christmas narratives – I'm struck by the swathes of silence. In Luke, once Mary has made her extraordinary *Magnificat,* she becomes, effectively, a silent figure. Perhaps the writer of Luke, writing in a prophetic rather than a literary voice, feels that the birth itself speaks enough. But it is as if the birth silences Mary. Equally, the baby Jesus is unconvincingly silent. There is no account of crying. Some will respond by saying that the lack of crying is irrelevant – after all, the gospel is not a novel, but a work of prophetic and apocalyptic literature. But still the absence of any reference to this basic human noise allows the space for the kind of sentimental Victorian 'Away in a Manger' Jesus ('little Lord Jesus, no crying he makes') to emerge. Except I do not read this silence as evidence of virtue; it is evidence of Christ's identification with the silenced. This is a God who has not yet discovered his voice. This unpromising, perhaps ignominious, beginning for God-With-Us is taboo-cracking, for what kind of God gets born in an outhouse? What kind of God invites the despised (such as shepherds) to his nativity? What kind of God becomes one of the silenced? In the beginning may have been the Word; but the Word in the Nativity cannot yet speak itself. I suspect some transgendered people will find their experience of being silenced most resonates with that of the so-called Holy Innocents; that their silence is not temporary, waiting to be overcome. Their voices have been cut off (by societal/ cultural/personal pressures) as permanently as Herod's victims. But that is not my story. My voice may be hidden, but I'm learning to speak. As Christ had to find his voice, so I am on a journey to find mine.

Life is different for me now and, inevitably, so is Christmas. When I woke up to the fact that public denial would not do, when I realised the unsustainability of grand gestures, I began the slow and sometimes painfully confusing process of 'changing gender'. It was a risky but ultimately correct decision. My family have been tremendously supportive and, perhaps, delightfully surprised – they have unexpectedly gained a sister, daughter and aunt. But the cost for us all has also been massive, and Christmas remains a kind of gathering up of both the joy and the cost. The joy lies in relationships reshaped and relaxed; in the discovery, in the midst of the ordinary annual gathering of family, of the absurd unexpected grace of God. Grace signified by the absurdity of God being born in an outhouse in Bethlehem among nobodies and the disreputable. The cost is wrapped up in a new kind of silence and a new layer is added each year. It is a silence no one in particular has made, but which impacts all my family, most particularly my parents. For one of the costs of my emergent identity has been to make it difficult for my family to speak confidently about my early life as a boy and young man. There is a sense in which, for my family as a whole, my early life has been lost.[4]

This is a kind of journey into darkness – a darkness that is just as positive as it may appear negative. The choices I have made have closed down certain possibilities – as all real choices do. However, unlike many choices people make, mine have closed down or at least made very difficult some of the discourses families take for granted: the chewing over and celebrating of all sorts

---

[4] As one friend has pointed out, this experience of 'loss' is perhaps far more common than many would prefer to believe. Families represent one of the key theatres of human living and thus will inevitably be the loci of some of our bleaker dramas.

of details of childhood. It is as if a light on the past, which most families take for granted, has been switched off. There is an absence. A silence. A darkness.

When I am in a one-to-one with my parents or siblings, things can be different. I have always tried to encourage my family members to feel they can celebrate (rather than feel shame about) my early life. I try to integrate my whole life into who I am now and recognise that there is much in my pre-sex-change worth celebrating – but the weight of being together *en masse* makes the public acknowledgement of my past difficult. This has particularly become the case when my siblings' children have been present – children who have only ever known me as 'Auntie Rachel'. I sense the difficulty in acknowledging my past has something to do with the social nature of Christmas: the present is important, but much of Christmas is memory and remembrance. Perhaps, in time, my family and I shall discover, like a delightfully unexpected present, a way through this new silence, this new darkness. And if we do not, then I'm encouraged by the thought that silence and darkness are not, in themselves, terrible things.

As for the Tonka truck of 1975, well, it is long gone, perhaps suffering the slow, stench-filled decomposition that plastic and metal experience in a landfill waste site. But in my head it is still with me, though I have become aware of how, in recent Christmases, I have been slowly dismantling this once indestructible toy, piece by piece, wheel by wheel, sometimes with care, sometimes with abandon. And each loosened bolt and nut is a making vulnerable, a loosening of false layers of identity, and a making space for God, the one who is easily silenced, to speak. As such, it is thus an embracing of God's darkness – profound, fecund, full of endless possibility and creativity.

One

Working it Out

Working it out[5]

Then a girl, a teen,
tangerine in cheap spray tan
clicks onto the bus
and sways towards the back,
her arse a rolling fleshy pendulum in retro jeans;
her ease in four inch heels, the hypnosis
of that arse she wields like a weapon,
playing with her body as if she were a
puppeteer adjusting a new doll's strings;
a girl trying out what it's like to be a girl
trying to be a woman.

Watching her from a distant evening
where I'm twenty four again,
conscious of those twin mounds on my chest
secretly raised over months, a pioneer
shovelling earthworks at night, afraid to be seen;
my stinging eyebrows thin as stiletto tips,

---

[5] This poem was originally published in *Magma Poetry Magazine* No
39, Winter 2007/08.

the too bright lipstick huge on my lips,
my eyes fixed ten feet ahead;
and I'm flicking my own weak tight male arse out
far and wide, side to side, picking my way
down the street as if to a metronome's click;
as if this will grow it fat and round as an orange.
Flicking it like a boy working out
what it is to be a girl working out
what it is to be a woman.

There is truly something extraordinary, horrifying and painful, in identity terms, about being 'caught between'. It is a land of shadows, of twilight, and sometimes of almost complete darkness. Perhaps many of us have had that kind of experience in some form or other – the experience of unemployment, say – but the trans person's experience can represent its very acme.

I have always been the kind of person who has sought out and been hungry for the applause of others. In some respects that no doubt reflects some essential aspects of my personality – which I've long since discovered are basically unshiftable – and my love of theatre and acting. I spent a huge part of my teens pretending to be other people on stage: Falstaff in *Henry IV part 1*, the narrator from Thornton Wilder's *Our Town*, Hobson in a radio production of *Hobson's Choice* and so on. I devoted endless hours to learning to play flash metal and rock guitar and loved playing the theatrical rock and roll 'star' on stage. And I was sufficiently talented as an actor – perhaps because of my need to cover myself with fantasy faces/masks – to be invited to join the National Youth Theatre.[6]

Like so many acting types, I've always been inclined to see the world as a kind of stage with me as a central actor who should be offered the best parts in all circumstances. This need for affirmation

---

[6] An opportunity I eventually turned down to pursue a chance to go and work in Jamaica.

has perhaps made me acutely aware of the slights, rejections and abuse that come when a trans person makes the decision to 'be true to themselves'. It also made my experience of being 'caught between' in those early months especially, and ironically, painful. For attention-seeker that I am, the last thing I wanted during that time of androgyny, was to be noticed – and to be laughed at and pilloried – for looking 'in-between'. For looking – to borrow the funny phrase used by the transsexual Barbara in the TV comedy *The League of Gentlemen* – like 'neither summat nor nowt'.

It is hard to forget that two-year period of my life. I began transitioning in 1993 – taking hormones, experimenting with dress, playing with my voice, trying to reconfigure my body. And, though I flatter myself that as a result of some natural gifts as an actor I was able to figure out what to do with my body, there was a huge amount of reconfiguring. The typical hunger of the trans person, especially in the early days, is to 'pass' and to be unnoticed. Sadly, that is not always possible for many transsexuals, even after years of transitioning. Nonetheless, if I was in some sense 'acting', I was basically improvising – and often improvising badly. I looked to other women's behaviour – their dress, speech patterns, body movement, all the things unconsciously absorbed since childhood – as my guide and then tried to work out how actually to live a life or (to borrow a phrase of Michel Foucault's) 'discipline my body' in unfamiliar ways. All this while seeking to live in reality. For this improvisation was not taking place on some protected soundstage, but while I tried to hold down a job and maintain my sanity. This was no mere 'theatre'.

I remember one particular sunny evening in about 1993 when I was walking down the main street in Lancaster. I have no recollection of what or where I was going exactly – probably to smoke some weed with a mate – but I remember one moment which summarised the cringe of being 'in-between'. I'd amateurishly slapped on a faceful of make-up, making me look (as one friend rather cruelly pointed out) like Jack Nicholson's Joker in the '90s *Batman* movie, and was wearing a loose mid-length blouse and some very tight black leggings. Max Wall would have looked classy next to me. And I was 'sashaying' down the street. I say sashaying – I was (as in the poem) swaying my boyish butt around in what was such a pathetic attempt at walking like a woman that someone might see it as a sarcastic parody. I was self-aware enough to know that I was hardly a plausible woman. My breasts had barely begun to form – all I had was an itch in the chest, a slight adolescent soreness. I suppose that at the time I thought that I looked ok or, if not exactly ok, that I simply had to get on with it. That is, having decided on my path, I just had to start living it.

To walk down that street – utterly conscious of my feeble attempt at public womanhood – even under the cover of night, took pretty much every ounce of energy and sheer bottle I had. I had to keep my face, my eyes, braced and staring ahead. The street – even if it was the main one – was basically clear of pedestrians, though such was my self-absorption that I barely noticed the few people there were. And then I spotted her. A young, pretty woman walking towards me, dressed simply in jeans and t-shirt, with long straight brown hair, moving with the simplicity and ease of someone who does not have to think about who she is. She seemed, to my anxious eyes, utterly whole, utterly relaxed – body and soul moving as one. The very opposite of me. I remember thinking, 'It is so easy for her.' I remember feeling that she was who I wanted to be. She was how I wanted to be. I remember her coming towards me and smirking. She didn't laugh. Our eyes met for the briefest moment and she smirked.

During that period of transition and ambiguity I experienced much worse than that smirk. I was living on quite a tough council estate and I got a huge amount of abuse from the local kids. Kids can be staggeringly cruel. I had things thrown at me. I had threats from adults. I'm just glad I was never beaten up. Some days I found it almost impossible to leave the house. And yet this woman's almost innocent, guileless reaction to how I looked and behaved stays with me and defines that period. Perhaps it was because that young woman symbolised all that I thought I wanted and thought I should be. It was as if the 'idealised me' was laughing at the 'real me'; the person I 'should' be (a kind of superego) laughing at what was actually the case (my ego). And my ego was slapped harshly about the face.

I could not live that time again. Some trans people claim they could not withstand sex reassignment surgery again; the experience is too painful. I'd happily face it again if I had to. It was so worth it. But I still sometimes dream of that transitioning time of ambiguity and it has the character of a nightmare. It became so clear to me that what freaked others out and, indeed, freaked me out was the convention-breaking power of androgyny and of indeterminacy. Being 'in-between' deprived those who looked upon me of ready-made, and mostly unquestioned, gender dimorphic categories – that is, of the unspoken visual assessment that 'x' is male or female. The simple fact is that we live in a culture that is conditioned to look for the 'either/or' rather than the 'both/and' or the 'not quite'. In philosophical terms one might say that being human is typically marked by an unthinking belief in The Law of the Excluded Middle.

At a personal level, during my time of extreme ambiguity, I felt deprived of the simple affirmation I was looking for: the visual and often verbal affirmation that I was a woman. It is interesting that I am now so very well established as a woman that I have no fear of playing with androgyny, but that 'play' is grounded in the simple fact that a) I know very clearly who I am at an internal level and b) I am clearly a woman playing with a boyish look. This does not freak people out like my appearance did in the early '90s. Then I was visually, verbally (I was playing with my voice, trying to find my female voice) and physically a human 'platypus', a seeming combination of incompatible bits; a bizarre boy-girl or girl-boy. I could not live that time again.

I felt deprived of a significant part of my agency. And the discomfort generated was in part chosen by me – at one level, I could have continued on with my usual male life and experienced the undoubted benefits of identity and power that confers. Even in our modern age, feminism is correct to point out that the male perspective is our default position. Being male confers an owner- ship of reality and a possession of public space which women, through social conditioning and the exercise of male power, are traditionally deprived of and have to fight to obtain. My moving into the world of ambiguity and the 'in-between' was a stepping away from self, into death and darkness. It was also a stepping into 'otherness'. That is, I took upon myself what is sometimes known as 'the Other': the one who is most definitely not seen as belonging to the dominant or normative groups and so can be dis- missed as less than fully human, or stereotyped as a 'threat'. It is a profoundly uncomfortable place to be, especially if one has a huge desire to belong. But much as I could not live it again, I now reckon that period as a kind of gift. A dark, uncomfortable gift. But a gift nonetheless. A gift from the dark, Living God.

Let me see if I can clarify. To feel as if one is losing one's agency and self, indeed feeling like one has become a kind of non-person, is uncomfortable and something most of us quite reasonably avoid. And yet it is revealing. At a head level – a level that gen- uinely matters to me as a thinker and intellectual searcher – there is simply no doubt that the experience of being 'in-between' reveals, in a truly visceral way, the extent to which our gender and sexual categories are constructed and are, in an important sense, arbitrary. I am not suggesting that these categories don't matter nor that simply through 'living as x' makes one a man or a woman. There is such a thing as an inner dimension to being a man or a woman. But there is simply no doubt that there is a huge perfor- mative dimension to who we are, shaped unconsciously from birth and which many people do not like having their attention drawn to. Part of the reason the gender ambiguous disturb many people is because they expose reality: rather than being like hard and fast mathematical laws, our identities – our human practices, behav- iours, beliefs and so on – are more like sediment thrown down on a river bed. This sediment runs very deep in places and is almost impossible to dislodge, but in others it is laid more thinly. This does not mean that the foundations of our gender and sexual identities are any less real or substantial, only that we should not imagine that gender is governed always and for ever by timeless laws. At the risk of sounding absurdly self-congratulatory, I want to say that for exposing this alone, gender outlaws are worthy of our praise.

If the above seems too highfaluting and cerebral, I invite you to consider the following. My journey into the 'in-between' will always feel like a dark, unsought-for gift because of its impact on my sense of compassion and generosity. It is very easy for many people not only to present their life stories as journeys primarily of triumph and success, with minor setbacks, but actually to experience the world in that kind of way. I may have been born into a working-class family, with the attendant social and financial disadvantages, but my upbringing was relatively simple and settled. And the kind of people I hung out with had mostly experienced such settled lives, though from a middle-class perspective. Our lives lacked the pain that comes from being on the outside or being alienated. These were easy, simple lives. And, since becoming a Christian, my experience of many people who end up as ministers has been similar. I'm sad to say that so many of those who minister are well-intentioned and lovely but lack any comprehension of life on the outside or edge. My life had, for the most part, been simple and smug. To become 'in-between' was a painful experience of revelation and alienation. To become the kind of person who is pointed at and avoided – even as this was softened by the fact that I had a number of wonderful supportive friends – was bleak.

And yet there is a kind of knowing that works only by suffering, by alienation and pain. It is easy to imagine that knowing things is an intellectual matter. Clearly that is true for many kinds of knowing. But it shows a failure of imagination to suppose that one can truly know love or tragedy at an intellectual level. Sometimes suffering is a kind of practical recognition or perception. That is to say, it is, for the sufferer, revelatory. It is an expansion of the world, partly constituting a person's correct understanding of her situation as a human being. This is the *pathei mathos* of Greek tragedy: the wisdom which arises from suffering. And this wisdom is no mere intellectual apprehension but a shift in our way of being. To journey into the 'in-between' was, for me, revelatory and deepening – bringing a shift not only in sympathy but in empathy and solidarity with the ridiculed, the broken and excluded. It was gift, but one that was unsought and one which in most circumstances most sane people would not choose.

Perhaps it has to be unsought. There is no direct path to compassion through pain and suffering. Pain in its many forms – psychological, physical, spiritual etc – is, in my experience, primarily nasty, brutalising and pointless. A sane person will – as a rule – naturally seek to avoid pain, exclusion and marginalisation. And the truth is that much of the time one's experience of such things does not constitute any particular kind of revelation. For example, when I have been lying on a hospital trolley in absolute abdominal agony it has been very far from a 'learning experience'. I have not been thinking, between agonised gasps, 'Well at least this is deepening my practical wisdom about suffering.' And yet there is a mystery here. The experience of passion may open the heart to compassion.

This is part of the glorious darkness of God. It is constantly tempting for people of faith to present the 'object' of their faith in a wondrous shining light – as a kind of divine 'vestal virgin', pure, unsullied and shimmering in white. And, in truth, there are plenty of images, not only in the Bible, but in all of the major religious traditions, to support something akin to this picture. But – even as it captures something many want to assert – it misses the deep mystery of the God in Christ. For the God in Christ is all about passion: he becomes our victim, handed over to us, the subject of our jealousies, fears and our desire to be in control. This is a God who gets filthy in the dust of Palestine. This is a God tortured at the end of a whip. This is a God who is mocked and killed. This is no clean, unsullied immortal. This is a man thoroughly caught up in and destroyed by the violence of the world. This is a man who is intimate with the world's darkness. And in this ironic world it is the perpetrators of violence who claim to be agents of light: the keepers of the peace, the protectors of the faith and the saviours of the nation. And on any human calculation these claims are reasonable: to wish to protect the nation from further violence or from one's occupiers is humanly commendable. These people are wearing metaphorical white hats.

It is only the one who is unafraid of darkness who embodies God's way. Christ is the one who discovers in the darkness the hope for the world and who takes the darkness into his being. He is the rejected one who travels down into the darkness of the dead, who walks in the company of the dead and the lost and yet is not completely destroyed. He is the one who takes death within himself and offers new life and hope.

We are not called to be Christ, but we are called to walk with Christ – to share in his story, his wounds, his life, as he shares in ours. To step into 'the in-between' and the attendant darkness was, for me, a step of both hope and pain. The hope of new life lay somewhere in that darkness, for the darkness was transformative. It was the darkness of possibility, like the darkness before the world began. And to have walked that path, I understand now, was a gift – a painful one, and one I should have preferred not to have received. Yet, such are the gifts from the Living God: they are gifts of life, not of ease and comfort. And in a world where so many are so readily scapegoated as 'the Other' and who suffer the depredations of marginalisation, I believe we need more, not less, people who can embrace the transformative power of darkness and come through changed and renewed.

Two

Learning to be Greek [7]

The Ancient Greeks knew a few things. Most of all they understood the way in which outside circumstance can compromise our decisions and how human flourishing – the living of the good life and the pursuit of human excellence[8] – is fragile. As the poet Pindar notes, '... human excellence/grows like a vine tree/fed by the green dew'.

So often that 'green dew' becomes acid rain. We readily imagine that our lives – grounded as much in luck (*tuchē*) as in reason and planning (*technē*) – are solid and unchanging. We organise our lives in such a way that we feel we are in total control and are insulated from the vagaries of luck or happenstance. However, there is a very real sense in which the more successful we are in that project of control, the less human we become: it is the very fragility of our lives that makes us human. If we are not changing and growing, then we are less than human. We are not, after all,

---

[7] This chapter owes an overwhelming debt to the philosopher Martha Nussbaum's seminal work on Greek tragedy, luck and ethics, *The Fragility of Goodness* (Cambridge: CUP 1986). My thoughts in this area are mere footnotes to hers.

[8] The term 'human excellence' can be misleading, suggesting an elitist conception of human flourishing; here I take it to mean being our fullest and most complete selves – our true selves. This has moral dimensions, but in a Christian sense is also about being in growing relationship with God.

called to be like the gods – unchanging, immortal, hard.

As shabby and flawed as many of my decisions have been, I have for most of my adult life, both pre- and post- becoming a Christian, had a commitment to human flourishing, both personal and social. My gender dysphoria has presented a very pungent experience of the way circumstance makes that very difficult. And, rather than Christianity, it is the Greeks – especially Greek tragedy – who have helped me chart a passage through this reality. I want to assert, along with Martha Nussbaum, 'that Nietzsche was correct in thinking that a culture grappling with the widespread loss of Judaeo-Christian religious faith could gain insight into its own persisting intuitions about value by turning to the Greeks.'[9] I may be a Christian, but I am not merely a Christian: I have been shaped in a world where Christianity is under severe question, and intellectual and personal honesty (given that I was trained as a secular philosopher and have spent a large portion of my life as a non-Christian) requires me not to rest on easy formulas of faith.

We are regularly confronted with situations in which we must choose to do or have either one thing or another. And often that is a choice between two goods rather than between the bad and the good. That was the situation I found myself in, in the early '90s: between trying to remain a man, and therefore faithful to one kind of story of myself (and all that went with it – family expectations and so on), and living as instinct and hope invited me.

It may come as a surprise to some that I present this as a choice between two goods. Perhaps many would expect me to consider the choice to pursue a public sex change as an unalloyed good and to write off my previous life. I cannot do that. I am singularly delighted to have had a sex change and I like to imagine this has brought benefits to others as well as myself; that (to put it pompously) I live a more 'excellent' life. I am, I sense, more relaxed and generous towards others and so on. However, my

---

[9] M Nussbaum, *The Fragility of Goodness* (CUP: Cambridge 1986) p.15.

choices – because they were real choices made from within a fragile human perspective – have been costly and compromised. Good things from my male life have been lost – friendships, the freedom from explaining myself and my story, a certain kind of liberty from censure and conflict and the 'ease' of pursuing, without too much interrogation, a career in acting, music and so on. For the things I have lost I feel genuine regret and I take this as an indication of losing a good or set of goods. I have gained much and yet I – and crucially others – have paid a considerable price. Whilst I run the risk of overstating the case and being self-indulgent – for I know very many people who have experienced far more significant losses and pain – I want to claim that, in a particularly Greek way, the situation I've found myself in was touched by the 'tragic'. Indeed, I want to claim that about the situations many of us find ourselves in all the time.

Aristotle famously tells the story of the sea captain who throws his cargo overboard in a storm to save his own and others' lives. He knows that he must throw it over and must act quickly; he sees the alternatives and makes the choice. And yet he was attached to his cargo and has a duty to protect it. He makes his decision – the decision only a fool would censure – and yet he will regret the loss of the precious cargo. Because of circumstance, he is left in a situation in which he has to choose what no sane person would ordinarily choose. Perhaps this conflict of good desires strikes us as somewhat trivial – for most would want, quite reasonably, to prioritise human life over physical goods. Sartre presents us with a more complex, human case. In *L'existentialisme est un humanisme*, he cites the famous case of the young man who, in wartime, must choose between his patriotic commitment to the Resistance and his obligation to his ageing mother. Such a case presents a genuine practical conflict, grounded in the complexity of human circumstances. Sartre's solution is to suggest that all moral principles are inadequate and that one should simply choose – with vigour, clarity and without regret. One should not allow oneself the indulgence of tragedy.

My own experience is that life is not as simple or heroic as Sartre presents. And even if one believes – as many philosophers from Socrates to Kant have suggested – that it is possible, through the exercise of reason, to come to a full and ordered assessment of the *one* correct decision, the simple fact is that our lived, embodied reality does not allow for such a God-like perspective. As we live we face choices, wrapped up in desire and ego and fear and hope, and we do our best in the face of conflicting options. And although Greek tragedy has sometimes been parodied as philosophically crude, its account of good people caught up in impossible circumstances is powerful precisely because it captures the truth of our experience. We may not frame our modern lives in the terms of Aeschylus or Euripides – in which people are trapped between the impossible and conflicting demands of the gods – but we know the cost of a choice between two goods. We know the reality of tragedy that leads not only to regret, but sometimes to the agony of remorse. Aeschylus presents a world in which Agamemnon, seeking to prosecute war against the Trojans, has an impossible choice. The war has been commanded by Zeus to avenge the violation of a crime against hospitality and yet, because of a violation against the goddess Artemis (to whom he also has obligations), the expedition is becalmed. Only the sacrifice of his daughter Iphigenia will guarantee the winds to carry the fleet. Agamemnon is caught between two horrific courses of action – impiety or the destruction of his daughter – and must decide.

When I finally went public with my gender dysphoria, in 1993, I was married. Frankly, my relationship with my ex-wife was already in a parlous state: my emotional and psychological wrangling about gender was a major factor in this, but not the only one. I find it very difficult to face that time, to hold it in my imagination and contemplate the emotional and psychological nuances. I am ashamed that I ever got married and placed my ex in the appalling situation of being married to someone as screwed up as me. I still feel like I betrayed her good will and used her for my own ends. I know relationships are two-way, and she was not perfect, but we married on false pretences, pretences fed primarily by me. Indeed, in a feeble attempt at honesty, early in our relationship, I actually told her that I just liked dressing up 'like a woman', that I was just a transvestite. I still wonder if this was a worse lie than if I'd kept my mouth shut. I had genuine affection for her but there was a real sense in which I was trying to prove I was a man and was using her for my own purposes. I was a coward for almost all of that relationship. It was only in 'coming out' to her that I showed any semblance of courage (and even that 'coming out' happened in the midst of an explosive argument, that is, when I was less than my best, rational self). My cowardice was so complete that when I tried to tell my parents about who I really was, one overcast summer day, I couldn't. My ex had to do it for me.

I've often thought of that day. How the four of us crowded into my parents' bedroom. How I sat on their bed crying and hiding my face. The panic on my mum's face. The calm of my dad. My expectation that my dad – always a powerful physical presence in my life, though not actually a violent man – would leather me once he knew the truth. The silence of waiting for tough and painful words to be delivered. My ex supplying those words. I've often wondered if my need to hide and my inability to speak was a sign of just how irrevocable going public was; of how terrified of exposure I'd become, even as I'd already made my decision. I'd been hiding so long – perhaps all my life – and the sheer weight of that past silenced me. When you've huddled forever in the dark – like the characters in Plato's allegory of the cave – how do you face the light?

I know, with hindsight, that in choosing the path of sex change I made the right decision. And, again with hindsight, it is easy for me to act as if it was the only rational decision. That it was, as our American friends put it, a 'no-brainer'. But to claim that breaks faith with the reality of my lived experience. There is simply no doubt that my marriage was on the rocks, but that does not mean that my life up to then was a write-off. There was substantial goodness, hope and possibility within it. And also immense fun. I had

– and not just in a hedonistic sense – *enjoyed* my life. As with anyone else, there had been times of difficulty, depression, fear and so on. But it did not have the character of pointlessness. Even if I had felt – at times – so appalled by my gender situation that I had contemplated suicide, I had and have no desire to reduce my life's character, up to that point, to one of a waste. Choosing such a radical change in my life – and at the time I could not appreciate how radical the implications of the choice would be – might have had the character of an imperative, but it was not free of substantial cost.

Greek tragedy again and again presents characters caught in impossible circumstances where they are torn by conflicting duties and goods. I've already mentioned Agamemnon – who ultimately commits the crime of killing his daughter as if she were a sacrificial beast – but one could equally cite the case of Eteocles, king of Thebes, son of Oedipus. He faces an invading army led by his brother Polynices. He faces a practical conflict between his obligations towards Thebes – which are very real – and his obligations to his brother as family member and with whom he has a shared past. Eteocles decides to 'face off' against his brother, seemingly unwilling to acknowledge the power of fraternal bonds, saying, 'Who else would it be more just to send? Leader against leader, brother against brother ... I shall stand against him.'

What is odd about both Agamemnon and Eteocles is that neither seems to fully appreciate the power of each conflicting obligation. Agamemnon becomes so convinced of the rightness of prosecuting the Trojan War that horrifically he embraces the slaughter of Iphigenia with the clear-eyed fervour of the fanatic. Equally, Eteocles seems to feel no psychological angst over the move to slaughter his brother – a man with whom he shares a close personal story and familial bonds. The horror expressed by the Chorus in each tragedy – and our horror too – lies in the lack of emotional engagement, pain and wrangling on the part of these tragic characters. The key dimensions of regret, and its potential corollary, remorse, seem lacking. This is only part of why they are condemned, of course: regret in itself would not free the characters from punishment for committing terrible crimes. Whilst being caught in impossible circumstances might foster our *understanding* for what they have done, killing itself is a sufficiently significant crime that moral censure remains appropriate.

My own appreciation of the situation I found myself in, in my early twenties, was sufficiently human that I experienced regret. However, I worry still about the impact of my actions: I fear that I killed, or at least attempted to destroy, my male self. And I sense that this action is worthy of moral censure. Perhaps I overstate the case. Perhaps I am being unnecessarily dramatic. That is, of course, possible: I am a notorious drama queen. But consider this: once I was set on my path of sex change, I ruthlessly sought to destroy all traces of my former self. I sought the annihilation of the person that had been called 'Nick'. And in so many ways I have been successful. And others – notably my family – have paid the price of my ruthlessness. Here are just some examples.

My family had known me as Nick for over twenty years. I had grown up in their company and been significantly shaped by them. Equally, my friends – many of whom I was very close to and with whom I'd shared most of the key rites of passage of youth – had known me for a good number of years. And quite suddenly I was trying to erase that person from the world. The last male thing I remember giving my parents was dressing up in a suit for my MA ceremony in 1993. After that I was ruthless. Even during the period before I changed my name legally I started insisting upon being addressed by female pronouns and being called Rachel by my family. They were kind and generous and tried to comply with my wishes. I was the opposite of kind: I would sulk and correct them when they used male pronouns or used Nick. My parents had named me and nurtured me and I bullied them, corrected them and cajoled them. At the time I considered it necessary. Maybe to convince people of such a radical change ruthlessness is unavoidable. I accept that, because of the hormones I was taking, I was undergoing considerable emotional and psychological shifts;

my moods were as unstable as a teenager's. As one friend pointed out, I went through five or six years of adolescence in one year. Nonetheless, in my desire to snuff out all references to maleness and to Nick I absolutely pulled no punches. It is perhaps a token of how much they loved me that they didn't cast me on the rubbish dump for emotional and psychological violence.

They loved Nick of course. And I destroyed him. My clothes, my voice, even my body, as it began to change, all were no longer Nick – the bearded, dreadlocked, skinny hippy with a love for drugs, heavy music and intellectual pedantry. For his sake, I guess, my family, and to a lesser extent my friends, put up with and loved the person I was becoming. Because I was their son, their brother, their mate. And yes, the person I was becoming was in utterly unquestionable senses still Nick – his history was mine and is still mine. And in the years since gender change I have had to come to terms with that and continue to try to reintegrate it into who I am now. But I killed that boy. I killed that man. I became Rachel.

Is it childish to think that, at some level, I should be censured for my behaviour back then? Not simply for being a beast towards my family, but for the way I treated the person I'd been and the life I'd had. If one accepts that my choice was conditioned in part by circumstances outside my control – my gender dysphoria was not, for example, something I've ever had control of – then my choices at least become understandable. I have felt regret, even remorse, for the way I've behaved towards my family and I've sought to give recompense and tried to be a better daughter. And I've felt regret for what I did to myself – to Nick, to my past – and for all that was lost, even as much was gained. The choice between two goods is always costly.

Christianity has – at its best, its most honest, its least cheap and most costly – always been unafraid of loss. Loss is inscribed in its very foundations. To return to my original point – I should like to believe that I have always had a commitment to human flourishing and to living the excellent life. Circumstances and practical conflicts make such a project extremely difficult, even as one seeks to cultivate virtues of love, courage and so on. We are compromised. We are people of unclean hands. And this is where the Christian story begins to help me comprehend my own story.

In Jesus Christ, God embraces a human life and shows us – in the dark night of rejection, of unjust violence, of the loss of his friends as they run away, and most particularly in the Cross – the mystery of hope and love. And most of all of forgiveness. In the loss of one human life, lived out in love, lies the hope of new life and the fullness of forgiveness. Even if my claim to be a killer is a little theatrical for most tastes, there is one truth I cannot deny: that the consequence of my choices has been loss. Not only for me, but for my family. So much silence has been forced upon them by my choices – about my past, my childhood achievements and so on. They – who still live in the area where I grew up – have had to endure whispers, innuendos and snide remarks about me from the locals, which I have not. Perhaps loss is the price we all pay for being human, for being beautifully fragile. Indeed loss is one of the key marks of being human. In order for us to be human, things must change, things will and must get lost; we have to lose them in order to have new life and new possibilities. But I feel that loss especially keenly. And – accepting that it may be merely self-pity – the regret sometimes nearly overwhelms me. However, the authentic human journey is always about loss and the possibilities of new life it opens. To put it another way, if the Christian life is about participating in the Divine Comedy, the actual living of it so often has the character of tragedy. And in the tragedy lie the pity, the hope, the weight and, sometimes, the beauty.

Three

A New Song

How do we learn to sing a new song when we've played only one tune our whole lives? And when we dare to take up another song, how do we cope when we discover that instead of the song of joy we thought it was, it feels like a song of lament, of pain and of loss? That instead of being a song of light and illumination it becomes a song of the night?

Becoming a Christian in my mid-twenties remains one of the most bewildering, delightful and mysterious commitments of an often rather bizarre life. If it is always difficult for anyone to gain proper purchase on the nature of their own life, then to comprehend this 'decision' feels, for me, endlessly slippery. This I know however: it has been a journey into loss and recovery, into false consolation and into real hope. It has been transformative, and by turns joyful and bleak. It has also been an encounter with the God that is living and a journey into becoming the person I truly am.

Jesus said, 'Those who seek to save their life will lose it, and those who lose their life for my sake will save it.' It is a statement with endless resonance, like a stone thrown into waters that generates infinite ripples. One ripple that many may miss – simply because they have had little cause to question their basic identity – is that in order to lose one's life, one must have one to begin with. That is, to give one's life to God, to lose it, one must have some sense of *who* one is to begin with. In order to lose oneself there has to be someone there to get lost. In a very important sense, it wasn't until I got into my mid-twenties that there was anyone much there to lose. I guess God had been waiting for me to 'appear' for over twenty-five years.

One of the effects of my ruthless attempts to divest myself of Nick and discover Rachel was that for the first time in my life I felt like I wasn't playing a part. The irony was that the person I had been for over twenty years – shaped and formed in a thousand conventional ways – felt increasingly like a series of masks, a theatrical invention. At the same time, as I 'played' with what it meant to be Rachel (the experiments with clothing, make-up, voice, bodily movement) I felt like I was becoming more myself. In the midst of the creation, the theatre and play, I was becoming a solid person rather than a set of masks. I'd be lying if I claimed that that time – even after the helpful shifts of living full time as a woman and of changing my name legally to Rachel in 1995 – was one easy march to self-realisation. But as I moved into my mid-twenties I felt like I was becoming the person I wanted to be. My life was coming together rather than fragmenting. For the first time I had a proper sense of who I was. It was hard fought for and hard won, an achievement of self-determination, with little encouragement from others. This was the context for my becoming a Christian.

Since my early teens I had consciously and publicly rejected God. Being an intelligent, status-conscious teen, I had regarded it as evident from an early age that being a Christian was not cool. My family was conventionally religious and it was expected that I be confirmed. I refused and began to cultivate an atheistic image (even though I was quite able at Religious Studies and genuinely enjoyed studying faiths). At university, when a Christian conference was held in my college, I put a large banner up in my building which said 'FUCK OFF CHRISTIANS!' My advanced education was entirely secular; the simple fact that philosophy had been practised by as many people of faith as not was irrelevant. 'Philosophy' as I was taught to understand it – whether in its Anglo-Saxon or European forms – was a secular, hard-nosed matter.

One of the curious things that happened as I became Rachel

was an emergent desire to pray. Frankly I found this mostly bewildering and at odds with my life. My life – as a student and teacher of philosophy – was about argument, about thinking, about advancing positions using logic and humour and reasoning. And, yet, forming within me was something more compelling than an argument – a desire or hunger to open myself to something which, my philosophical training suggested, was essentially absurd. It frightened me. Just as a control freak becomes terrified of what will happen if they let go of their temper, I was frightened about what would happen if I let go of my use of logic. I sensed that if I did so, I might lose myself again. And after fighting so hard to gain a proper sense of myself, surely I would be mad to let that go? In letting go of myself I had this fear of becoming a drone, a dupe, a kind of faith-driven robot. And this invitation to prayer felt exactly like that: an invitation to let go of control of myself, of my power and self-assurance, of me as the centre of my world. Of me. Having worked so very hard to establish these things in trying circumstances, to feel drawn to let them go was not especially attractive. I had worked so hard to gain a sense of myself and now I felt an invitation to throw that sense into the void.

In hindsight, it is possible to discern an interesting human/psychological pattern in this desire to pray and there is no need to make any reference to 'spiritual' things like grace, Spirit or God in order to explain it. During that period of my life I was engaged in a massive effort at control: I was using whatever means were at my disposal to conform my body and mind to my deep desire to be a woman. This process involved, in the face of ridicule from those who didn't know me, considerable energy and focus. For becoming a woman was about finding myself and becoming more relaxed, but ironically this entailed massive amounts of focus and energy. And, it might be argued, in the face of that effort at control, a psychological analogue emerged – the desire to let go of control.

As far as I can see, this is not an unreasonable conclusion. What intrigues me is that the desire to 'let go' took the form of prayer. Rather than going on a massive drug splurge or wanting to run naked into the sea or suchlike, I felt drawn to prayer. And not just to pray in some conventional sense – that is, as a kind of talking to God, an unburdening that may also involve asking for things. I knew all about that kind of prayer. When I was about twelve or thirteen I'd pray every single night – the same litany of fears and hopes. Praying that there'd be no nuclear war, praying that my dad's asthma would get better and, most of all, asking that when I woke up I'd be a girl. And when I became a proper teen, I put away such childish things. God, I decided, doesn't work magic. This desire to pray was different: this was a hunger to be still. To listen. To 'be' rather than to 'do'. To allow my carefully managed life to be consumed in silence. And more than that, to take the risk of seeing whether that silence was pregnant with hope and love.

Some things are irresistible. At Whitsun 1996 I was staying at my parents' when I simply could not resist any longer. The urge to pray was overwhelming and I let go. I remember saying, 'God, if you are there, then I am yours.' And as I dared to lose control, I sensed God was there. I felt like I was letting go of my carefully shaped control. Of my carefully crafted self. And I felt absurdly loved – utterly, unconditionally loved. For exactly who I was.

There have been many occasions since then when I wish I hadn't been. This encounter has perhaps been more disruptive than any other experience or decision of my life. As a result of it I've annoyed and even lost friends, I've left jobs, abandoned plans and ended up pursuing a vocation that has often been as much a frustration as it has been a gift. As a result of that encounter, I have been forced to face up to some deeply unpleasant aspects of myself and, perhaps most annoyingly of all, have felt called to a life of self-acceptance and community reconciliation. Life was so much easier when I didn't have to reckon with a God who not only loves me but actually likes me too.

Inevitably, being a questioning sort of person, I've spent a fair amount of time – especially during those initial bewildering days when my faith was extraordinarily raw and vibrant – asking myself if this stepping into faith was merely a search for comfort. One of the standard parodies of faith is that of the 'comfort blanket': of the creation of an all-encompassing, all-powerful figure (usually a father) who offers reassurance for the insecure and the needy. Only a fool would dismiss this possibility out of hand. Given the emotional disruption I'd experienced as a result of gender change, it is hardly beyond the bounds of possibility that I would want to invent a comforting flight from the reality of living. And the fact is that, at one level, I sense there may be some truth in it.

The real question is this: is it possible for a number of seemingly incompatible things to be true at the same time? In my days as a hard-nosed philosopher, committed to the Law of the Excluded Middle, I'd have to say 'No'. As a Christian, living in the midst of the paradox of Jesus Christ (as the one who is wholly man and wholly God), I am inclined to say 'Yes'. So, while there is no doubt that I experienced a singular event in 1996 – an awareness of intense love and affirmation that threw my life up in the air – it is open to any number of interpretations. Here are some I would not wish to deny.

There was an erotic dimension to this conversion experience. Many have commented upon the relationship between sex, death and religion, for they share a common theme – that is, the 'nihilation' of the self. The power of sex is its capacity, in ecstasy, to wash away our sense of self; religion – especially in its ecstatic forms, but more broadly as it connects with spirituality – has equally sought the loss of self in union with God. And death. Well perhaps that is the ultimate loss of self. (At the risk of being excessively tasteless, I would say it is certainly pretty final.) To experience, in that moment of surrender to God, the loss of 'letting go' was intensely erotic, deeply sexual even. Does that make it inauthentic and thoroughly questionable? Only if faith is reduced to some sort of intellectual matter that excludes our whole embodied selves.

Actually, I suspect this is a far more common experience than many people are inclined to acknowledge. The language of many Evangelical-Charismatic choruses – what some people have amusingly called 'Jesus is my boyfriend' songs – certainly suggest that this is the case. And I was someone who was starved of sexual confidence. Indeed, I had barely begun to come to terms with what it meant for me to be a sexual being now that I considered myself a woman. Perhaps it was inevitable that in allowing myself to be out of control for the first time in a very long time, and given that human sexuality is about far more than mere sex, it was hardly surprising that the experience had an erotic dimension. Spiritual and sexual *ekstasis* are closely related and this was undeniably one dimension of my experience.

The sense of union with God that many of the great mystics have spoken of has often had that character. Mechthild of Magdeburg, Hildegard of Bingen and Julian of Norwich are all mystics unafraid of Divine Love as a burning passion. As Mechthild has God say in *The Beguines*, 'Your heart's desire shall you lay nowhere/But in my own Sacred Heart /And in my human breast.'[10]

Equally, I certainly would not wish to deny that, at the point of my conversion experience, I was vulnerable. Yes, I was lucky to have a number of good friends (though sadly many of those who'd known me primarily as Nick had slipped off the radar), I was enjoying an interesting and demanding role at my university and I had a supportive family. However, I remained under considerable stress. Changing gender just *is* stressful. Although my appearance was far more in line with how I should have liked it to be, I was still negotiating a serious anxiety about how others saw me. I still had a genuine horror of being 'spotted' and labelled as a 'tranny' and therefore as 'a man dressing up as a woman'. I was uncertain in many of my relationships and, though I felt increasingly at peace as Rachel, I cannot deny that in discovering God – and with it, God's affirmation and unconditional love – I discovered an extraordinary peace. It would take very little psychological skill to construct a scenario in which my faith in God was merely the result of a deeply seated, and beautifully sublimated,

---

[10] Mechtild of Magdeburg, *The Overflowing Light of the Godhead*. 1.43

need for acceptance. This is the image of a child searching for love and acceptance and discovering in her imagination the made-up friend who gives it to her.

Nor would I wish to deny the importance of the sense of belonging that my new-found faith gave me. This was not simply about now feeling able to join a church congregation; this was the deeper sense of feeling as if I had begun to find my place in the world, what I perhaps might now call being part of 'The Kingdom'. It has not escaped me that, as someone who through massive doses of hormones had gone through a second adolescence, wanting to belong to something might have been really important. Like so many adolescents – even one doing it again in their twenties – I might have found the need to be part of something greater irresistible.

I cannot pretend that in those early days there were not aspects of my nascent faith that were childish and almost fantastical. Several years later, in an attempt at reconciliation with a friend I'd seriously annoyed as a result of my overbearing evangelical zeal, I described that initial stage as like falling wildly in love or in obsessive lust. I struggled for weeks, perhaps even months, to be able to think about anything or (more significantly) anyone else other than God. He – in the person of Jesus – was all I really wanted to talk about. I wanted to spend all my time with him. I wanted everyone to know him as intimately as me. In short, I was a total, overbearing, selfish idiot.

This image of the fired up Evangelical-Charismatic – which is certainly what I became for a while – is precisely the image of the believer that many within the church are almost inclined to present as the ideal picture of the Christian. But during that period I was not myself. I was living in a bubble. I was a hyper-self. If Christianity is about exposure to reality and truth, then I was over-exposed. In the very least I had not begun to integrate the implications into an ordinary, lived life. To put it another way: I had indeed given myself to God, but I was yet to receive myself back. I was very glad for sensitive, intelligent Christians like the university chaplain who directed me to works by the likes of Bonhoeffer, which enabled me to begin to process the rapid period of change. In time the fury cooled and I managed to find my way back to myself – re-formed in the light of faith.

God provides us with what we need. There are circumstances where that is almost impossible to believe. Indeed in which perhaps it is impossible to believe and, if we dare, all one can endeavour to do is seek to affirm it as true. But I sense that, as absurd as my behaviour became, the extraordinary power of my conversion experience was the condition of the possibility of my faith. I know many people of faith whose experience of 'conversion' has been gradual or gentle. My own was dramatic. But this was a gift: without a profound encounter there simply was no way I would have been able to trust in God. Who I'd become, who I'd made through need, desire and sheer will – Rachel – was simply too precious to me. There was a hardened carapace of self-willed creation. Without a moment of pure crisis, of dazzling darkness, I could never have let go of my grip on that self.

At that time I was seeing a gender identity psychiatrist of US origin. When I told him I'd become a Christian, he smiled, and in a Californian burr told me he found this interesting, but that in his experience all transsexuals who'd 'found God' returned to their original gender. Perhaps his experience of Christian transsexuals had been limited; perhaps his experience was limited to the more conservative, ultra-Protestant Christian culture in the US, where belief in 'reversion therapy' for queer people is more common. My experience was quite different – it was one of affirmation and acceptance, not condemnation and rejection. And while this might again be parodied as wish-fulfilment, I take it as a token of encounter with the Living God. For my expectation – pre-conversion experience – had been of condemnation. How could God accept a freak like me? One dimension of my fear of letting go was the fear of rejection. I should have preferred to avoid this prayer of casting myself into the beyond of God, but it was ultimately irresistible. And instead of rejection I received overwhelming, bewildering, unexpected love.

How do you begin a new song when you've sung one song all your life? I had had a pretty conventional English childhood: Church of England primary school, a life in which God had been very far from central, in which I'd learnt the Lord's Prayer but that was about it. From my teens onwards I'd happily lived with minimal reference to the Christian God and actually thought of faith as gauche and childish (something which, if I'm brutally honest, I sometimes still feel). My song was, even after the changes of my early twenties, still an essentially conventional one in which religion and God didn't really matter, sharpened considerably perhaps by a life lived in the midst of hard-nosed philosophy. A new song became possible only because of Love. Since the time of St Augustine, Christians have spoken of 'prevenient grace' – the grace which goes ahead of and before us. The instinct to pray falls into that pattern, but it was the encounter which was transformative. And in that encounter was recognition, hope and the first flowering of redemption. I was beheld by God and I was beloved; and I beheld God, encountered love and surrendered. God comes to us as the ultimate stranger, for we can barely imagine perfect love, and most of all, in our deepest selves, we can barely imagine that love being lavished on us. The new song was startling and beautiful and fantastical. I want now to look at how it became terrifying, dark and challenging. In short, I want to look at how it became real.

Four

Into the Desert of the Real

I have met some born-again Christians who act as if, in order for the modern church to be given new life, we need only to recover the passion, the vibrancy and hope of the Acts of the Apostles. That if only we could live as those first disciples and apostles lived, we would truly be welcoming the Kingdom. For we would be Spirit-fuelled faith heroes, propagating the faith with the courage and energy of Paul. As beguiling as this way of thinking might be, it is ultimately false: it imagines that the Book of Acts is straight history rather than – at one level – propaganda. The growth of Christianity in the Mediterranean Basin was slower, patchier and more interesting than the propaganda would have us think. Nonetheless, I genuinely understand the enthusiasm for the born-again way of thinking because I've lived it. In those first wild months of newly received faith, as I settled into life in an Evangelical-Charismatic church, made new Christian friends and so on, I felt those possibilities. The world, for me, was aglow with Spirit and wonder and all we needed was a radical simple trust in God in order for the world to embrace Christ. My relationship with God was simple, easy, loving and intimate. And – as I see it now – of little substance. The time had yet to come to know the real God – the Living God, the dark, mysterious and hidden God. Or to put it better: yes, I had encountered the Living God, but in an aspect only suitable for a child. It was the milk of faith rather than the meat.

It is always exciting to feel as if one is at the centre of things and part of a movement of hope. It is – for so many of us, perhaps the more insecure among us – a thrill to belong. This is the power of cults, especially for the likes of teenagers who perhaps above all others feel the need to be part of something. It is also the power of certain kinds of revolutionary movement whether sick perversions like Nazism or timely protest groups like CND in the 1950s. As someone who had gone through an accelerated second adolescence in my mid-twenties, I felt the new hope that comes when one feels one has found a home. And yet there was no depth in my relationship with God. Let me put it like this: When we first fall in love there is often a staggering intensity. Perhaps no one quite knows just how intense those feelings can be except for the young. And yet this is not the fullness of love. Love is shaped over and through time. It is costly. It breaks and reshapes us, and is full of longing. It completes us and yet draws us on as we search for more. It is the heart of God.

My problem at that time was my sense of feeling full of power, of feeling like one of God's chosen, his blessed ones, my sense of being almost Teflon-coated and unstoppable. But the truth is that our human life, to repeat an earlier point, is not only fragile but at its most human and beautiful when it embraces its fragility. We are not called to be gods, but to work out our faith and hope in fragile, flesh bodies so easily damaged and so easily diverted from their course by circumstance. As such we are called to be people of character rather than flashy impressive acts. God himself did not come to us in Christ as a superhero, as Superman, solving all our problems through his superior strength and so on. He came to us as vulnerable as any of us, and as readily destroyed.

In order to begin to step into a genuine relationship with God – in order to sing the song of love I'd been given and discover that at its most true it is as much a song of pain and lament as of joy – I needed church. It is almost too obvious to note that the church reflects both the very best and the very worst of us, for – whatever else it is – it is composed of human beings. And human beings are sometimes hopeful, sometimes seek after petty forms of power and sometimes are mobilised into the most remarkable sacrificial acts. Becoming a committed Christian meant for me becoming committed to a church and (given my vaguely Anglican upbringing) I reached for the only tradition I knew – the Church of England. And in the midst of an Evangelical-Charismatic expression of that church one kind of picture of God and one kind of image of myself began to die. The God who I thought I knew fell away like the idol he was. And as he fell away so did one idealisation of myself. For who we imagine God is and who we imagine ourselves to be are intimately connected.

In the midst of my growing confidence as a woman and my sense of genuine affirmation from God one dimension troubled me: my sexuality. As a reasonably sophisticated academic I was quite able, intellectually, to make a distinction between gender and sexuality. And it remains self-evident to me that to assume that a person's gender dictates their sexuality is crass and simplistic. Equally, I had, since my teens, a decent number of friends who were gay or lesbian or bi. Nonetheless, at a personal level, I was troubled. I had, as a man, basically been attracted to women. My emotional attachments (for I was not especially interested in the mechanics of sex) were towards women. I had had a number of girlfriends and had even got married. As I pursued sex change, my sexuality got more complicated; I was aware of ongoing attractions towards individual women but I also opened myself up to being attracted to men. It is fun to speculate whether this was partly a hormonal matter, or a willingness to embrace a latent dimension of myself given the shift in my social status, or simply a desire to experiment with traditional female roles/identities. The fact was that, then as now, I fancied, even lusted after, certain men. However, my primary orientation was towards women.

To be a woman who loves other women is – it goes without saying – rather tricky in a conservative Christian context. While I was a member of my first church, it went through a mini scandal in which a minister had to leave because he was actively gay. I felt immensely torn about Evangelical attitudes towards gay people: intellectually and culturally, it seemed absurd to condemn or criticise a whole bunch of people just because they loved people with the same secondary sexual characteristics as themselves. Love is just too rare to condemn. And yet, in the rule-driven and selective-biblical approaches of my church, being gay was clearly a problem. And 'the narrow way' meant you shaped up or shipped out. And somewhere in the midst of this conservative thinking was me. At one level, I felt like I belonged. I sensed and loved the energy of this church, its passion, its willingness to accept the power of the kind of personal conversion I'd known. Its sense of movement. And yet I was so very different from its normative picture of human beings. A transsexual. And someone who, even as a woman, loved women. Who began to see herself as a lesbian.

During that time a very good non-Christian friend likened me to a Jew who wanted to join the Nazi Party. The point of his some-what over-egged rhetoric was that the Christians would love my sincere faith, but hate (even persecute) my gender dysphoria and sexuality; whereas my liberal, secular friends would embrace my gender and sexuality but despise the religion. In truth, I was sur-prised to discover how readily my conservative Christian friends accepted my gender change. My vicar and his wife were very sup-portive. But the elephant in the room was my sexuality. No one wanted to talk about it, except in the most conventional forms. When I spoke of fancying some bloke, everyone was cool. But I daren't mention the truth and the complexity. This was Christi-anity as arch-conventionality, in which nice men love nicer women, couples don't have premarital sex (or if they do, they keep quiet about it), get married, make children and live happily ever after, blessed by the Lord Above even when the reality of human desires and experience, as in my case, was very different. For in this context, it was the humans who were flawed and must change, not the religion, the dogma or the doctrine. As in all authoritarian ideologies, it is the person who is in the wrong, not the system.

We all have snapping points. And sometimes, if we pay attention, this is a moment for reality to break through, that is, for God to embrace us. I was sat in church one Sunday evening in 1997, probably about a month before the General Election. None of my usual cronies were there, but by that time I knew enough people in the two-hundred-strong congregation not to feel 'on my own': my guitar skills had been put to good use in any number of worship groups and, as a result, I was 'known'. The preacher was talking about the election and how we had to search our consciences in order to vote wisely as Christians. Somehow he got onto the subject of sexuality, though I simply cannot recall how he tied this in with the politics of faith. And then he was having a go at 'homosexuals' and how their behaviour was immoral and so forth. How they must repent and turn away from their sinful lives. I'd heard similar things whispered at this church, but nothing quite so direct. And, as I sat in the pew, I found myself crying. Not loudly. Not sobbing. But tears were running down my cheeks. I have no idea if the women sitting either side of me really noticed or cared. They certainly didn't respond. And I felt the urge, in the middle of the sermon, to get up and walk out and never come back. I didn't even feel the urge to challenge this man. All I wanted was to leave in silence and never return.

It remains one of the key, unavoidable questions facing gay or, as I now prefer, queer people within the church: do we remain or do we leave? On any number of occasions I've come close to walking away. I've often reflected upon that night – did I stay because, rather like a woman beaten by her husband, I was so damaged that I'd rather take the abuse than have no attention whatsoever? So many queer friends are both intrigued and bewildered as to why I stay, indeed work, within the church. Even more so when I say that I do so not simply to try to change it from within, but because, as furious and frustrated as I get, the church – in all its hypocrisy, human craveness and prejudice – remains a place of grace. And remains a place of grace because God is bizarrely and wonderfully passionate about the freaks, the half-mad, the second-rate and yet glorious bunch that we – the church – are. And if God can still value the loons within it (including me), then so can I.

Nonetheless, that night was a kind of end, even if I didn't appreciate it fully at the time. Looking back I am convinced that the Living God was vibrantly active that evening, perhaps far more so than in my somewhat theatrical conversion experience. But I sense he was not active in the vile words of the crummy sermon (except perhaps in the most ironic way). He was not in the over-heated worship songs complacently celebrating how much each of us loved God and God loved us. Perhaps he was not even in any obvious way in the prayers of the people. He was in the silence of those who were unwelcome. He was in the absence of those this church considered unacceptable. He was in those we complacently allowed to be written off. He was in the tears. He was in that part of myself that, for the sake of trying to obey some narrow rule and fit in, I'd neglected, was afraid of and would not embrace. That night he was not in the successful, the powerful and the faithful, but in the discarded, the despised and the lost. And he was not even a 'he'. 'He' was as much a 'she' as anything else. And if he was in the sermon, then it was as an ironic gift: the hateful words of the preacher turned upside down so that it was possible to see the truth – that God's Love is for the outsiders and outcasts.

Everyone has a breaking point. And given what I had already faced through gender change and the years of chronic illness that were about to begin, that night in Lancaster was not, in one sense, a huge slight. But it was a key moment in returning to the Real, to the Living God. I've met some remarkable, committed Evangelicals, and I am also conscious of the way in which their movement has become increasingly engaged in social action and how, privately, many question attitudes towards sexuality. The church genuinely benefits from their commitment and passion. But my experience of Evangelicalism was of a movement that sincerely, lovingly and blithely fed two closely related idols within me – a false God and a false Self. And one way it did that was by saying,

'Because of x, y, and z in the Bible (especially sections of Paul), this is exactly what God is like and this is how you must understand Jesus.' And this is a God who, if he is merciful and loving, is also one who has very specific and detailed behavioural requirements of his children and, given how some church leaders talk, is absolutely obsessed with those requirements. This is a God who is often stage-managed away from abundant welcome, unconditional love and radical forgiveness into 'You're welcome as long as you measure up to these rules and conventions'. This is church as holiness cult, afraid of our creatureliness – our bodies, our desires, our brokenness and our fragility.

Most of all, this is an angry God who requires a payment of blood in order to appease and satisfy his injured sense of justice. This substitutionary approach to atonement appeals to the ordered, analytical Evangelical mind. It is perhaps worth outlining how this approach runs. Broadly all versions are variants on the following: In the beginning, God created the earth and it was good, but then we messed it all up. We fell, because of our choices, into sin – a great sin against God's infinite mercy and justice and goodness. Because we mucked up the world, there was no way we could put it right; indeed God would have been perfectly within his rights to destroy humanity. But God's mercy got the better of his anger. He came up with a solution. For whilst his infinite mercy may have allowed him to let things rest, his infinite justice demanded that payment for Sin be made. Only an infinite payment would do – something only God could offer. But here's the problem: it was humans who fell in the first place, so the payment had to come from the human side – otherwise it wouldn't be a real payment.

So God came up with this cunning plan: send his Son into the world as a man so he could pay the price – since he was human he could fulfil the human requirement; because he was God he could make an infinite payment. And that payment was made by the Cross. The full and sufficient sacrifice. A blood sacrifice of the Son covers the sins of those who choose to follow him.

It is a neat and ordered picture. It is a tempting picture. It is a bloodthirsty picture. It is an appalling picture. And it is an idolatrous picture. And part of the reason I sense it is idolatrous is because I don't think it actually changes us; it's something to be understood, it's a theory. And, as such, it is 'God' according to our image (that is, defined by our idea of a God) – a God as managed and as controlled as the Baals and the Golden Calf of the Old Testament. If the Cross is to matter it must change us and most especially change our hearts; and that's why I think the picture I've just given gets it almost entirely wrong.[11] The angry God who needs appeasing isn't up there in 'heaven'; that's not God. The angry God is us. The angry, jealous, wrathful God beats within us. Demands a victim. It wants to make a victim of queer people, or any other group/person who does not measure up to the normative rules of the dominant group. And perhaps even if we belong to a scapegoated group we can also search for 'victims' on which to project our anger and sense of righteousness.

To the question 'Who killed Christ?' the answer surely has to be that we did. Those men and women who gathered on that night before the Crucifixion to condemn Jesus represent us. They demanded a victim, an innocent, to make things right – to ensure that business could go back to normal, that human hearts would not have to be changed by love, that the status quo could be maintained. The only kind of God who wants or needs a blood offering is us. The bloodthirsty God whose hunger is only appeased by the death of his only son haunts our imaginations. It is the kind of image that can keep us as frightened children; keeping us in bondage instead of liberating us.

---

[11] One of the reasons that the Eucharist matters so much is that it is all about encounter and transformation. In faith, we meet and receive Christ. There is a deep physicality about the act and mystery of communion. And most of all it is an act of resistance against theorising. Certainly there are many theories of 'the meaning of the Eucharist' and there is a place for them. It is important that we reflect upon our faith. But the key moment in the Eucharist is a mysterious encounter that outruns the desire for understanding.

And so the easily stage-managed God, or at least one face of him, began to die and something richer – the God of the excluded, the despised and so on – began to form. The idol had seemed so alive but it had ultimately only been the glamour of human control – of being able to cast God in our/my own image. And, of course, to claim that he had 'died' makes walking away from that image of God sound too easy. He continues to lurk inside me, and probably all of us, because he is the easy God, the one we can make up and cower behind. He is the puppet we can use to hide from our true selves and from the Living God. But the death-blow had been struck, and with it a death blow to a certain picture of myself – the one which meant I could simply cut out huge aspects of myself and claim I was doing it in order to be faithful to God.

I find it ironic that someone like me – who for the sake of 'self-acceptance' and the desire to be 'whole' decided to become a woman – could end up pretending that God (and by extension the church) required me to deny and not accept other key truths about myself and then call that 'wholeness'. It was as if the following had happened: I'd journeyed a certain distance into self-acceptance on my own; then I'd encountered God who initially I'd experienced as accepting me fully; and, finally, once I'd begun to walk with fellow Christians in the church, I'd decided, 'Ooh, well they don't seem to like *that* bit of my identity and they can prove that God feels the same way, so I won't accept that bit of me either.' Clearly, this is an over-simplification. Even so, it is easy to blame the church and its picture of God and human beings on this analysis. And, yes, the church must take its share of the blame for alienating individuals from God and from themselves. No matter what its redeeming features, for as long as the church continues to mess with and turn the minds and emotions of the vulnerable against themselves, it can expect many to turn their faces against it.

However, I was guilty too. Yes, I wanted to belong and feel part of something, but even if being part of that church entailed denying truths about myself, in choosing to belong to it I also received many longed-for goods. It fed my sense of being part of an exciting movement of faith, in which the Spirit was alive and blessing people. And, perhaps most excitingly for my ego, blessing me. I felt special and incredibly alive. I felt Teflon-coated and powerful. If that night of tears broke the golden back of an idolatrous god, then it also lay open the illusion of my bullet-proofed self. It was a beguiling fantasy to imagine that, in the strength of God's Spirit, I was some sort of warrior of faith. The truth was that I was a vulnerable, ordinary human being as broken and unresolved and unfulfilled as anyone else. The illusion of feeling untouchable, unbreakable and Spirit-charged was just another sign of not facing reality; of wanting to be in control and assured. Of not relying upon God.

It would also be an over-simplification to say that after that curious night in church when I sensed God speaking, I simply walked away, full of self-acceptance and so on. Life does not work like a computer program – we do not live in binary but as confused and confusing flesh bodies. But nonetheless it was an end. And a new path began to emerge. A fertile path. A path that led further into the desert's darkness.

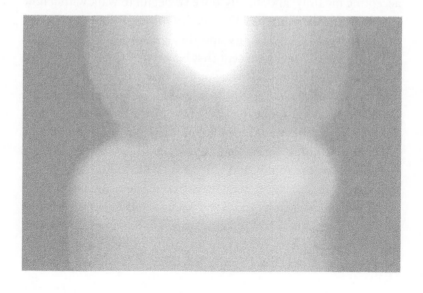

Five

Getting Naked with God

One of the most dreadful and yet wonderful truths of the Christian life is that it is not so much about being built up as stripped away. It is about exposure. It is about nakedness. It is about getting naked with God. And not being ashamed. Being in the company of God is not, in any conventional sense, about being safe, consoled or blessed. And, in my experience, accepting that truth is both deeply troubling and profoundly hopeful.

By early 1999 I was living a life of new possibilities. I was in a fun, happy relationship with another woman. I was living and working in Salford, having moved there in late 1997 to live in a base Christian community and do community work. I was about to see an examining chaplain for Manchester diocese in the hope of being recommended to go for selection for priesthood. I felt confident, affirmed and settled in my life as a woman. It had been a huge wrench to leave Lancaster and its intellectual challenges, but as my sense of vocation had emerged and an increasing urge to serve among the excluded and marginalised had developed, I'd taken the risk of moving. And though life in Salford was often extraordinarily tough, edgy and challenging, it felt like home. I felt like things were coming together. I was realistic about my vocation: I still thought it was pretty unlikely that the church would be brave or bold enough to recommend me for ministry training and yet I sensed it was not beyond the bounds of possibility. My world felt more solid and secure than perhaps it ever had. I guess that's how it often feels for those who build their homes on sand.

The examining chaplain – whose job it is to advise the bishop on who should go forward to a selection conference – told me that the church was not quite ready for me. She concluded that even if she suggested I go forward for formal selection, she knew there was no way I'd be recommended for training for priesthood. She felt I was intellectually and theologically interesting, very articulate and with a decent spread of practical experience, but I was just not settled enough. Which I suppose was one way of saying I was too 'unstable' both as a Christian and as a woman. It was not a message I wanted to hear and I felt angry and singled out. I was probably very childish about it. In hindsight, though, there was considerable truth in her conclusion. My Christian faith was only a few years old and my journey into womanhood was not quite complete. And yet who wants to be told, in effect, that they're unstable? A more acute problem, however, intervened almost immediately.

Since 1997 I'd been having increasing problems with my health, specifically with my digestive system. For the most part I'd been coping. I'd decided it was just Irritable Bowel Syndrome. Yes, I was going to the loo up to ten times a day, but so what? So what if I knew the location of every single public lavatory in Salford and Manchester? That didn't mean I had a really serious underlying problem, did it? And then my bowels totally stopped working. I was admitted to Hope Hospital as an emergency and operated upon immediately – the first of countless operations and procedures as a result of Crohn's Disease.

If Christian faith is about a kind of progressive exposure to reality and becoming one's true self in the company of the Living God, the two or so years which followed that emergency surgery were the most significant of my life. They were sufficiently significant that I can only think of that time as a kind of death. The process which had begun in Lancaster with death blows to particular images of God and self was, in many respects, completed during those two years. One kind of picture I had of myself and of God died. At the same time I began to learn to be me in a new way and discover within it the character of resurrection. I had to reckon with a more loving God. And, as I will suggest, a more uncomfortable one. For as Belden C Lane so potently puts it, 'God's grace comes sometimes like a kick in the teeth, leaving us broken, wholly unable any longer to deny our need.'[12]

During most of those two years I was significantly ill, both physically and psychologically. In late 1999, after months of investigations and operations, during which I lost a lot of weight and strength, I chose to have a colostomy. For someone who had had significant issues with body image, this decision was, to say the least, very difficult. I was terrified that it would compromise my relationship with my partner, that it would make her love me less. I was terrified that my body – already difficult for me to accept – would become utterly repellent. It was a sign of how low and ill I'd become that I chose to have a procedure that I associated only with old people at death's door. In fact, my partner was incredibly supportive and she helped me to make a wise decision. Yes, it was a challenge to adapt, but it was successful enough that it began to give me back my life. It became part of me and I've never looked back.[13] However, to come to that initial decision was difficult and for many months afterwards I still struggled to regain any sort of strength and energy.

During 1999 I also became unable to work and lost my job. I was forced onto benefits, and although my partner had a reasonable job, the financial and emotional hit on top of feeling permanently ill was stressful. Equally, I was just beginning to process the implications of the Church's 'no' to my ongoing exploration of

---

[12] Belden C. Lane, *The Solace of Fierce Landscapes* (Oxford: OUP 1998), p.32.

[13] Indeed, I cannot now imagine not having a stoma. In 2004 my initial stoma stopped working as a result of progressive disease. This was replaced with a temporary ileostomy. In 2006 I chose to have another colostomy formed. When my colon was overwhelmed with Crohn's in 2008, I had to have a permanent ileostomy.

vocation. I was angry, confused and bewildered by the changes in my life. I grieved for what I sensed I'd lost.

I spent a lot of time shouting at God. Indeed, the situation I found myself in definitively showed me the extent to which faith – mature or otherwise – is a visceral matter. Intellectually, it genuinely was no problem for me to say, 'God is not to blame for the situation I find myself in. God is not into punishment and being a Christian is not an insurance policy against suffering.' And yet emotionally I felt (to be blunt) shat on by God. In one form or another I spent much of the time saying to God, 'How can you do this to me? What have I done to deserve this? Why me? I thought you loved me?' Theologically, I felt ashamed. Emotionally, I felt entirely justified. I was a beast to live with. My partner must have really loved me. I was a confused, angry mess who looked and felt awful. And that was without including another factor that was busting me apart.

In 1999, after years on the waiting list, I hit the top of the list for sex reassignment surgery (SRS). In those days the process of getting to the point of surgery was extremely slow. NHS transsexual patients were inevitably, and perhaps understandably, low priorities in an underfinanced system. And finally after four or so years, my time had come. The time I had longed for and had gone through countless meetings with psychiatrists for. It was to be my time for confirmation, in which who I had become would be confirmed by a radical and longed-for operation. And I was simply too ill to have it.

I was shattered. I felt somehow silenced. It was as if my narrative – the journey towards the longed-for SRS that I'd waited and worked for, the active life of service I felt called to, the health I'd reasonably taken for granted, given that I was young – had been wiped out. I felt like the journey of hope I'd begun in Lancaster, and which had led to Salford, had come to nothing. The fertile land had turned into desert. I did not cope well with being silenced. I retreated further into myself. I tried to speak to God – in the midst of the anger – and I tried to pray. I tried to listen. I tried to keep speaking to my partner, to listen to her, and tried not to be a total bitch. I slept a lot and came very close to being clinically depressed. I drew upon the remaining energies of youth to keep the show on the road and, because personal strength is never really enough, I failed.

Muslims believe that there are ninety nine names of God. I believe God has countless faces and countless names. And, insofar as she is a God who provides, she provides those names and faces which are sufficient for hope. The face of God I found waiting for me in the depths was a darkly beautiful and terrible one – the suffering and forsaken God, crushed and despised. And, at that time and place, she was sufficient if not to save me, then certainly to stop me from falling further.

In a previous chapter I spoke of the substitutionary account of atonement. It is a picture of salvation which relies upon the Cross and the crucified man/God. And yet if it is a theory which draws close to the mystery – the power of the crucified, suffering and forsaken God – it misses the point entirely by turning it into a theory. For this is not a face of God to be understood but to be experienced. The point is this: who is the God who saves? Christians like to say it is the God of Love. And inevitably such statements lead to countless parodies from secularists and humorists alike. For this God of Love is presented as seeking to change human hearts by being a rather kindly and gentle and generous chap, perhaps rather like the ineffectual but well-meaning vicar of British sit-coms. And this soft God is seen as no match for the demands of the real world in which humans face complex, compromised decisions and can scarcely manage their competitive and acquisitive instincts. If this God is about calling us to our best and most excellent selves, he stands no chance, even if his intentions (and those of his followers) are good. And quite how this God can speak into the depths of our worst experiences is bewildering. For it would be like a well-intentioned fool offering tea and sympathy to someone who has been tortured, in the belief that such an action is going to make all the difference.

Or perhaps the God of Love really looks like the superhero who saves the day through special powers, through strength or super-human endurance. This is the God who demonstrates love by doing stuff for us – getting us out of scrapes, making the world better by repairing our relationships, saving us from falling build-ings, evil men or our sins. The immortal cartoon character Homer Simpson captures this picture of God perfectly when he says, 'I'm not normally a religious man, but ... if you're up there, save me, Superman!' Now, this, it has to be said, would be a useful God. This is the kind of God that people would understand. It is one reason why we, as humans, are both constantly fascinated by and creating superhero figures (in comic books, films etc). And some-times in the way we talk about Jesus – as the one who takes away the sin of the world – we see echoes of this way of thinking. But as appealing as this picture is, this is the God who requires nothing of us. This God does and we are passive. We are not changed in ourselves except that, at best, we are grateful. This is the God who takes away our agency, our fragility and the reality of compromise.

Neither the rather lovely and ineffectual God nor the super-hero God will really do as the God of Love. Not if that God is truly to meet us as we are and, through that encounter, we are to grow ever more into the likeness of God. I do not deny that there are times when the face of God may be experienced as 'lovely' or 'super-heroic'. That is, it is possible to encounter God in kindness and joy and warmth and in friendship; it is possible to encounter God as the one who saves us from our sins. But Love's true trans-formative power lies in the depths of our humanity: in our essen-tial fragility and capacity for brokenness and the prices we pay for being limited, passionate creatures. The God of Love is found within, rather than as either some external power or a kindly voice seeking to change us.

In the midst of my own distress – which comprised the worst set of experiences I'd known until then – the God who came to meet me was the God of solidarity, who shared my life, my vulnerability and my story. This was Love as the One who was simply alongside me, sharing and holding the pain. And, somehow, through that solidarity began to transform it. It was not clever, or intellectual or theologically impressive. It was simply real. It was Jesus Christ found within: the Love that is so outrageous that it becomes a human, fragile and breakable. Easily tortured, damaged and destroyed.

I cannot quite explain how God's solidarity is transformative. Perhaps that's the point: the love which stands besides us, which bleeds with us, and will not walk away is beyond explanation. 'Explanation' is the business of theories and analysis. Transformation is about experience. This I know, however: the love which came to me was costly. It was dark love. Sacrificial love. Why do I say 'dark'? Because this was love that is only truly known in the difficult places, in a world where our usual strategies of control and success have failed. God did not come as a lightning bolt of grace lifting me up out of the pit with wondrous light and power. I found God in Christ squatting beside me in the darkness. And the point is that this love as solidarity is not some light in the darkness; it is actually part of the darkness. It waits for us. Christ – the forsaken, the suffering one – who is faithful unto death, waits to meet us in the countless deaths that any of us can face in this life.

It is reasonable to ask, 'What is the hope in such a picture?' For there is no doubt that the Christian faith is a resurrection faith: that is to say, the perspective from which we are invited to understand Good Friday is always Easter Sunday. And I do not doubt that and I shall try to say something more theologically nuanced about the Christian Hope in a little while. For now I simply wish to acknowledge that – from my experience at that time – hope really had the character of holding on and – when that failed – of seeking to trust in the company of the suffering God. And there were times when my strategies of holding on failed. But when I fell further into the pit, he would fall with me. And together, one day, we would be raised.

Sometimes the church has talked of Christ's 'harrowing of hell'; of how, in being crucified and dying, Christ went down into the land of the dead and defeated death. It is found both in major creedal statements and perhaps most famously in Dante's *Inferno*. Virgil, the guide, indicates that Christ, 'the mighty one' rescues the Hebrew Forefathers. The notion of Christ's descent to hell is perhaps a little medieval for modern tastes and, yet, there is power in this metaphor. For part of the deep but dazzling darkness of God is that he too has walked in the company of the dead. Death does not destroy him. He walks through the paths of the dead, in the company of the dead, into new life.

John's Gospel talks again and again of the 'third day'. Of how on the 'third day' God acts: in the turning of water into wine, in the raising of Lazarus, and, definitively, in the resurrection of Jesus Christ. My experience and that, I think, of many who have felt ripped up by life is that that 'third day' – at a personal and social level – can be a very long time coming. In so many ways I should prefer to forget those two years of my life. At their best they were like two years of Ash Wednesdays – chastening, austere, uncomfortable, exposing; at their worst they were too many Good Fridays. And yet, they were gift. For our God is a paradoxical God: in the midst of death is life. And the way of our deaths is the way of abundant life. Who would choose to meet this Living God who comes to us in our defeats and pain and losses? Only a fool. Or someone who cannot avoid him. As my health and my hopes began to break down I tried to run. That is to say, for as long as I could I tried to remain positive and tell myself, 'Well this is not so bad. If I just keep going today, something will turn up. Things will soon be back to normal.'

And that person died.

It is so tempting to try to turn Christian faith into a kind of morality and talk about the need for Christian values. The Way of Christ is not, first and foremost, about correct behaviour. It is about the death of self and, in the midst of that death, receiving life, thereby helping us to become who we truly are. All of this will have implications for how we live; but it is really about who we are. It is about transformation and discovery.

It is about meeting the Living God.

Interlude One

Often it is fiction rather than theology that better enables us to tell the truth of our experience. As I shall explore more fully in the next chapter, during my initial experience of ill health I began to write. The following is one of the results of that time, written in about 2000. I include it in some trepidation because as literature it isn't much good. It is also something of a period piece: I do not think I could write it now, nor would I want to – it strikes me as too crude (and I am not referring to the swearing) and formulaic. But I think it indicates better than a chapter of academic prose where I was as my health and confidence fell apart. It indicates the kind of God I was searching for.

The Bleeding

As he went, the crowds almost crushed him. Now there was a woman there who had been suffering from haemorrhages for twelve years; and though she had spent all she had on physicians, no one could cure her. She came up behind him and touched the fringe of his clothes, and immediately her haemorrhages stopped. Then Jesus asked, 'Who touched me?' When all denied it, Peter said, 'Master, the crowds surround you and press in on you.' But Jesus said, 'Someone touched me; for I noticed that power had gone out from me.' When the woman saw that she could not remain hidden, she came trembling; and falling down before him, she declared in the presence of all the people why she had touched him, and how she had been immediately healed. He said to her, 'Daughter, your faith has made you well: Go in peace.'

She couldn't remember which she'd heard first – the rumours of a young Rabbi healing the sick and bringing good news to the poor or the story of the bleeding woman who'd suddenly been healed by him. It didn't really matter. She'd taken note. Perhaps it was what people said about Jesus – about how he wasn't afraid of being close to the unclean, the untouchables. Perhaps it was just the fact that someone else, with a curse like her own, had been healed. After all, people like her didn't get healed. Yet everyone said that it had happened. So she'd begun to hope. And she knew she had to seek out this man, hardly a difficult task even for an outcast like her. All she had to do was listen to the words on everyone's lips and follow the word of mouth until it drew close to him. For whether they loved or hated him, everyone was talking about Jesus.

At first, she couldn't make him out. A large crowd was following and surrounding him. Overwhelming him, she thought. If he's there. She realised she had no idea what he looked like. What was she doing here anyway? This was no place for her – with people, with clean people, whole people. What was she thinking of, coming here? Of course, he'd take no notice of her – what man ever had? She was outcast, unfit to be with men, unfit to be a wife or mother. No one came near her – not even women, for fear of getting her curse. No, this was no place for her. She should go. But as she was leaving, she caught sight of him – just the back of his head, but she knew it was him. And she had faith and knew she could go on. She started to push her way through the crowds, shutting out the indignant words spat her way, pressing on towards her goal before her faith ran out. Until he was there, so close she could touch him.

'Get back, woman' – a voice, then a man's face aimed at her. 'Don't bother the Rabbi today,' he continued. As he said this, another man she just knew was Jesus stopped walking and turned to face her. Incredibly, like an army under orders, everyone else stopped too. Stopped and seemed to turn their attention towards her. Jesus said, 'Andrew, leave her alone.' Silence. Or so it seemed. All she could think was, 'He looks so tired.' Tired and troubled. Like her father had once looked when she was a child – the look of one waiting for the debt-collectors to come and take everything. She didn't know what to do. She wanted to speak, to ask for mercy, but all she could do was stand before him quietly crying. He opened his mouth, as if to speak, moved forward, as if to hold her, but something stopped him. And instead of words of peace or an embrace of welcome, he looked into her eyes with a gaze she could not fathom. Mouth half open. Tired, painful eyes. A look that seemed to mark the beginning and end of all he had to say to her, for as he gave it he began to draw back and turn to go. Leaving her standing there. Leaving everyone puzzled and silent. And as he moved, they moved, leaving her alone on the road. Humiliated. Confused. Unclean. With nowhere left to go.

Nowhere left to go. 'Bastard,' she thought. 'How could he do it to me? What kind of a person does that? In front of all those people. Surely not a Messiah. Not a king. Just another man with a following. A magician who'd run out of tricks. He'd nothing to say. In front of all those people he'd nothing to say. He couldn't even touch me. Why couldn't he touch me? Why couldn't he care for me? Why couldn't he heal me? If even half the things they said about him were true, he could have healed me'. She just wanted to be well and she'd had faith. He could have made her well, but he didn't. 'Bastard,' she thought. Humiliated in front of all those people. Where could she go from here? Run after him down the road? Confront him? But what was the point? She'd never get anywhere near him, not this time, and anyway she'd be a laughing-stock. The one he wouldn't heal. Too much shame. And how could she go back home? It'd be even worse. Yet where else was there to go? It offered shelter, at least. She was tired. She'd dared to hope, she'd acted in hope. Her hope had died. She went home.

Home. A hovel away from the clean and good. Yet it wasn't much of a place for hiding. For as the truth got out, that she'd been to Jesus but not been healed, the mockery became more nasty than any she'd ever known. Mothers singled her out, frightening their children with tales that they'd end up like her if they were bad or faithless. Not just outcast, but cut off from the mercy of God. Even those who were like her, the unclean who lived around her, kept their distance and shouted insults. This faithless woman. Until she hid herself from others more completely than ever before, filling her time rearing the hate and anger that had been born to her on the road. Tenderly nurturing the spite fathered by Jesus. Aimed at Jesus. Waiting for Jesus.

And wait she would, sensing hate, like a tumour, growing within her; but the waiting time was shorter than she'd imagined. The opportunity for revenge arrived, like a fever, unexpectedly and barely announced. For the 'King of the Jews' had pushed his luck just too far. In front of all the wrong people in the city down the road. Because he just couldn't resist riding in triumph into Jerusalem, provoking the Romans and the religious with his grand claims, and disrupting the life of the Temple. But, like all false Messiahs, his cause had burnt itself out, the crowds had turned against him and he'd been arrested. 'Joy,' she thought, 'he's going to be crucified on a rubbish dump outside the city wall.' This she had to see. Had to be part of. If only there was time. So she asked God to grant her this moment of blessing, that she might play her part, that she might watch him die.

Oh, happy day! Happy day. It was so long since she'd felt like this. Like a prisoner set free, like the blind man given sight, like the child she'd once been. No stumbling for her today; today was her day. Her life would be her own today. For one day. Yet, in the end, after her urgent journey, the rubbish dump crucifixion wasn't quite how she'd expected it to be. For she couldn't muster the dignified entrance she'd planned, so hot and sweaty had she become. Nor was there much of a crowd; just a few women and soldiers and passers-by. And the two others nailed to crosses. A poor audience for a denunciation. And she hadn't expected the place to feel like this. Like decay. Like winter earth getting ready for a new crop. Most of all, she hadn't expected to feel this scared, to feel that she could lose her nerve at any moment. She thought she would laugh she was so out of her depth. Quietly, she approached his cross.

It was a commonplace brutality. A hundred petty fanatics had ended this way. But, in meeting him like this, she could barely cope. He was a naked, failing, blood-and-shit-oozing piece of sweat. Marked out by nails, already dead, even if each shattered breath insisted otherwise. His was a bruised face and closed eyes created by skilled, unseen hands. Surely he was beyond sense. And she felt like she was carrying a message she could barely own – long since memorised, worn down, no longer her own. 'Perhaps if I start,' she thought. 'If I get it over and done with.' But what was the point? He was little more than a corpse. No point in screaming at a corpse. Bastard. He'd got away, again. Anger flowed up within her like a spring of living water.

'Bastard ... you complete fucking bastard,' she screamed, 'you piece of shit, you lying piece of shit, just die, just get on and die ...' On and on, she screamed.

Slowly, Jesus raised his head and opened his mouth as if to speak. Painfully, he mumbled something like, 'Father, forgive them for they know not what they do.'

'What's that?' she said, 'Forgive them? Forgive me? You arrogant shit. It's you who should be begging forgiveness. After lording it over others, for playing at being Messiah.' Her voice dropped. 'For what you've done to me ... what you didn't do for me.' She fell silent, then almost to herself, 'Why couldn't you heal me? Why me?' She began to cry. Undignified. Uncontrolled. An ancient, animal pain breaking the surface.

Eventually, she looked at the cross again, expecting, hoping he'd be dead. That would be some sort of end, at least. But he wasn't. He was looking at her. She was sure of that. Not the look he'd given on the road; he couldn't muster that. This was more of a glance through a half-opened eye, but he was looking at her nonetheless, she was sure of that. 'Got your attention at last, have I?' she thought. 'Well, fuck you. I don't need you. You're not a saviour; you're just some piece of shit on a cross.' Still he looked at her. Through dying eyes. No longer waiting for the debt-collectors to come and take everything. They'd been and gone and this mess on the cross was what they'd left. Still he stared. On and on as if he daren't let go. This effort directed at her. Reaching out to her, demanding that she mustn't let go. All she wanted was for him to die. To just let it go and die.

'You don't understand, you can't understand ...,' she cried. But she was exhausted and couldn't carry on. She couldn't keep this anger up any longer. For there seemed nothing more obvious, now, than that this man understood as much as anyone what it meant to have everything stolen away from him. A theft felt as keenly as her own. And in these moments of death he was sharing the last of his life with her. With her whom all had ignored for so many years. Sharing his final moments of life with someone who wanted him dead. Somehow, she felt like she was dying too. It was dark. She was on her knees, still bleeding, still unhealed. In front of her, a man was dying on a cross. Perhaps just another madman bleeding to death. But together they bled, through wounds that would never heal. This was their meeting, and as this man quietly died, she sensed that in her bleeding he might always be with her.

Six

Finding a Voice

How should one imagine resurrection? Clearly there are a number of familiar pictures. Inevitably and appropriately, for Christians, our first instinct when we think of resurrection is to go to Jesus; and when we think of the *Eschaton*, the Christian hope in the New Heaven and the New Earth, we typically apply that bodily resurrection to wider humanity. Clearly, however, it is a term with wider application. If we think of organisations or corporate bodies – a football club say – we will think in terms of their bouncing back from near annihilation to future success. For those of us who have experienced significant personal lows, perhaps we see 'resurrection' in terms of a return to self and confidence. What if resurrection, in that latter sense, were actually akin to finding a voice? For if death can take many forms then surely one of them is the experience of being silenced. Being silenced is one of the ways in which our agency is taken from us and when our agency is stripped away we are caught in a kind of death.

It is almost too obvious to say that the world is full of silenced people. The voices of the poor, of women, of children, of gay and lesbian people and so on have always been ignored and pushed to the margins. Equally, it is a common experience of those who have been the victims of abuse and violence to feel stripped of agency and voice. As Brita Gill-Austern notes, '… for persons who have lived under structures of inequality, domination and control the experience of feeling silenced is a common phenomenon.'[14] And then there are people who, through the corrosive effects of chronic illness, depression or mental ill-health, feel excluded from the discourses which might empower their lives. Elizabeth Stuart, speaking in a specifically queer context, notes, 'Depriving people of language with which to make sense of their experience is a particularly effective way of keeping them silent and disempowered.'[15] What is true in that context speaks as powerfully into countless others.

Being chronically ill was corrosive. Being unable to have sex reassignment surgery because my body was a wreck was bruising. And trying to make sense of feeling that God was calling me to ordained ministry and yet being told the church was not ready for me was bewildering. It was so hard for me not to think that the church's view was primarily based upon its suspicion of me as a trans woman, that is, upon a kind of institutional inequality. Circumstance stripped me of the means properly to articulate what was going on. Who I had imagined myself to be began to seem a mirage. In the silence I searched for sense. In the silence there was – I discovered – still God. In the silence, there was still the possibility of the Word.

It is one of the great clichés that people who face serious adversity in life start writing, whether that be poetry or autobiography or fiction. There is now a whole sub-genre of literature, populated by titles like *A Child Called It* or *When Daddy Comes Home*, devoted to survivor stories. Such writing is often disparaged as vulgar and exploitative, but it is hardly surprising. When one has experienced the effects of silencing, either by circumstance or by

---

[14] Brita Gill-Austern, 'Pedagogy under the Influence of Feminism and Womanism', p.153 in Bonnie Miller-McLemore & Brita Gill-Austern, eds, *Feminist and Womanist Pastoral Theology*, Nashville, Abingdon, 1999.

[15] Elizabeth Stuart, *Daring to Speak God's Name*, London, Hamish Hamilton, 1992, p.10.

the cruelty of others, there will be a hunger to speak, to make sense, to articulate. Like countless others before and since, when faced with difficult circumstances, I tried to write. And, I now see, this was not just a matter of finding words for my experience, but of beginning to find a voice. This process – ongoing, shifting and growing – is a kind of resurrection and therefore of journeying further with God.

As a result of illness, unemployment and loss of confidence I was in crisis. How I saw myself – as an active, 'successful', capable Christian, a trans woman on her way somewhere and so on – had come into real question. In the midst of this personal crisis I had to find a new way of going on.

As I began to write – sincere, appalling poetry in which I mistook heartfelt sentiment for quality, and short stories which sought to articulate my emerging sense of God – I discovered, to my shock, the extent to which my voice had never really been my own. For as I wrote – crudely, personally and sincerely – I saw the gap between what I was trying to do and where I had been. I had never previously stopped to think about the extent to which my written voice before this splurge of creativity had been that of the male-dominated Academy. During my late teens and twenties I had been educated and initiated into the Western academic tradition, studying and ultimately tutoring university-level philosophy. One might imagine that this experience was precisely a process of empowerment and liberation. Yet this enculturation into academia, which I had sought as a way of escape from limited social opportunities and as a way of expressing myself, eventually became stifling. Rather than discovering my voice, I learnt a useful style.

This new process of writing – of beginning to find a voice – revealed just how little the academic voice had been mine. And, although I continue to use the academic style as required, I came to understand that in making an analytical style my primary voice I had really been adding a layer of self-silencing onto my life. For I had grown up as someone whose voice – as a trans person – had already been self-censored. And the more I wrote, the more I recognised that though, in my early twenties, I'd taken the massive step of giving my transsexual self licence to speak and be known, I had never dared to reflect properly upon what that voice added up to. My whole twenties had been driven towards becoming a passable woman, towards convincing the medical establishment that I was sincere and for real, and ultimately towards confirmatory surgery. And now – because of illness – I was forced to stop. At last I had space to discover who I was – as Christian, as trans woman, as lesbian, as a person hungry for my own voice – in the midst of all my changes.

Adrienne Rich, writing about her experience of a lesbian relationship, suggests:

> *we're out in a country that has no language*
> *no laws, [we're chasing the raven and the wren*
> *through gorges unexplored since dawn*
> *whatever we do together is pure invention]*
> *the maps they gave us were out of date*
> *by years ...*[16]

Though writing about a relationship, her picture of pioneers needing to discover a whole new language and explore beyond the bounds captures my experience brilliantly. As I began to wrestle with how to express who I was and had become, I realised that if I'd ever had a map or a key to myself, it was as out of date as the *Mappa Mundi*'s take on the world. Rich's most famous poem, 'Diving into the Wreck' – which is about diving into the history and myths of the world and finding a great absence, the absence of women and gay women in particular – concludes:

> *We are, I am, you are*
> *by cowardice or courage*

---

[16] Adrienne Rich, *The Fact of a Doorframe, Poems Selected & New 1950-1984*, (New York: Norton, 1984), p.242.

> *the one who finds our way*
> *back to this scene*
> *carrying a knife, a camera*
> *a book of myths*
> *in which*
> *our names do not appear.*[17]

I had been stripped down by circumstance. I had been becalmed and forced to ask who I was. Yes, I had re-encountered the God of Love as the one who suffers with me, but I was still a wreck. And in learning to write, in seeking my own voice and searching for who I might be, I had to dive into that wreck of myself to see what I might find. And I found, definitively, that I did not fit into the conventional stories and myths I had sought for so long to place myself in. I could not be the nice Christian woman that I'd tried to be. And in recognising, at a deep level, that I did not fit, I began to accept fully the complexity of my sexuality and my identity as a lesbian and, most of all, began to celebrate it. I began to realise that I could no more play a conventional stereotype of what a woman should be than I had been able to play at being an authentic man. I began to explore with more freedom what God might look like to an unconventional creature like me. I began to trust myself and I began to trust God – God liberated from unthinking tradition, religious rules and theological convention.

The spiritual masters have always known that how one sees oneself is close to how one sees God and vice versa. It is one reason why spiritual directors are typically keen for directees to explore their own story and place their prayer life in the wider context of their lives. In diving into the wreck of myself I was exploring who I was and therefore how I saw God; in being exposed to the God of solidarity and pain I had to figure out what that might mean for who I was going to become. To put it another

---

[17] Op cit. p.164

way: it is easy to picture 'salvation' and 'resurrection' as something done to us (by Homer Simpson's superhero god), but actually we are invited to be participants and partners in these works of life and creation; we are invited to find words, become story-makers, to weave our story into God's and let God's story be woven into ours. I needed to find, perhaps invent, a new language. I needed poetry. I had entered into a process that was about discovering my own voice, a process in which I continue to engage now. It is a path which, as Eavan Boland so aptly puts it, is 'a forceful engagement between a life and a language'.[18]

It should come as no surprise that in searching for my own voice I should turn to poetry. For in searching for words I was looking for the way to express myself both precisely and yet in ways that enabled me to reimagine and reformulate myself. Poetry is incredibly precise but powerfully suggestive. All art is liminal – that is, it stretches and extends the possible ways we encounter and comprehend the world. Poetry does this by precise and startling word craft. Words shape and create worlds. As Nicola Slee notes, poetry 'witnesses to the transcendent, to the beyond in our midst, to the "more than" that beckons human beings beyond the immediate, the functional needs of the moment.'[19] It is, then, in an important sense, 'useless'. As Ogden Nash amusingly notes, 'Poets aren't very useful/Because they aren't very consumeful or produceful,' yet precisely because poetry is not involved in a utilitarian exercise it has the power to speak into our deepest possibilities. Poets' words, at their best, create suggestive effects – effects which may draw attention, among other things, to 'the transcendent' in our midst. David Constantine puts it succinctly

---

[18] Eavan Boland, *Collected Poems*, Manchester, Carcanet, 1995, p.xii. I take Boland's words a little out of context (which refer to her wrestling with her Irish/cultural inheritance and her life story), but they speak powerfully into my life.

[19] Nicola Slee, *The Public Use of Poetry*, Audenshaw Papers 215, 2005, Hinksey Network, p.1.

when he says that poetry is 'a widening of consciousness, an extension of humanity'.[20] And while in an obvious sense it does that through the very precise, carefully crafted and startling use of words, it also achieves that effect through its 'silences' – through what it does not or refuses to say. Through its curiously useless work it enables folk 'to sense a reality of which they might previously have been unaware'.[21] The search for my own voice has been a search for words – unexpected, edgy, world-shaping, life-transforming. But it has also been an attempt to pay attention to the creative silences.

Finding my voice – that is, becoming a poet, understood both in the specific sense of a writer of poems, but equally in a broader sense of being someone alive to the possibilities and power of language and its transcendent effects – has rested upon a kind of gentleness and patience: a willingness to wait. Not merely in the sense of waiting for words to emerge, but also a waiting upon God. And, to return to my theme, this is a kind of 'darkness'. It is an acceptance of what I want to call 'The Dark God'. Henry Vaughan famously wrote, 'There is in God, some say/A deep but dazzling darkness: as men here/Say it is late and dusky, because they/See not all clear./Oh for that Night! Where I in Him/Might live invisible and dim!' In that fecund darkness – the darkness which holds the countless possibilities of creation, its pregnancy – there is the heart of God and the spring of the poetry our lives might offer. This is the God we cannot use for our purposes and devices, for deep darkness consumes us and denies us the means to chart our way. It leaves us 'invisible and dim'. We are liberated from our own convinced powers of control and talent and mastery.

And yet finding a voice – as an invitation from God as much as a human need and desire – must also entail a searching for sense.

---

[20] Cited in Neil Astley, ed., *Staying Alive: Real Poems for Unreal Times*, Tarset, Bloodaxe Books, 2002, p.18.
[21] Slee, 2005, p.2.

The writer of John's Gospel invites us to embrace a simple truth: 'In the beginning was the Word and the Word was with God and the Word was God.' The fecund darkness of God is also the Word being spoken and given and received. The poetic voice, even in the silence of waiting, has not been silenced, but is active, giving and searching for sense. It is an encounter between world and word. Rowan Williams captures this rather beautifully in the poem 'Emmaus' when talking of the 'solid stranger' who 'fills up' the pilgrims as they walk the road:

> *So it is necessary to carry him with us,*
> *cupped between hands and profiles,*
> *so that the table is filled up, and as*
> *the food is set and the first wine splashes,*
> *a solid thumb and finger tear the thunderous*
> *grey bread.*[22]

World and Word meet and are broken open in revealing possibilities both utterly grounded and yet transcendent; thunderous and yet ordinary. The poem concludes in beautiful, dark and ambiguous consolation – 'Now it is cold, even indoors/and the light falls sharply on our bones/the rain breathes out hard, dust blackens/and our released voices shine with water.' Our faithful, honest poet-priest Christ offers us nothing more or less than the truth. And it is not comfortable and rarely comforting.

The emergent voice I recognised as mine was not safe. Nor was the God of whom I wanted to speak. For my voice was a voice that spoke from the margins, proclaiming a marginal, troubling God. And this was a voice of liberation. One way of looking at this is, again, through the prism of Love. In personal terms, I had experienced this kind of trajectory: firstly, God as enfolding love – as unconditional love; secondly, God as the one

---

[22] Rowan Williams, *Headwaters* (Oxford: Perpetua Press, 2008), p.21

who suffers alongside; and, then, God as the one who both gives voice to the excluded, the broken and lost, but is also in that voice. And each of these images is a horizon of Love, in the midst of other horizons. But this God who gives voice to the excluded and is in their voice is troubling and uncomfortable – both personally and socially. For the first time I properly embraced a love which suggests that not only are trans people, gay people, the chronically ill and so on the beloved of God, but that God *is* trans and gay and chronically ill and a woman and everything else.

That is to say, I found myself in a place where I not only understood in a visceral way the notion of God's priority for the excluded, silenced and vulnerable, but also needed to articulate an expansive conception of God. The Christian church has legitimated certain ways of talking about God – male, fatherly, monarchical and so on. Such ways of talking have been so dominant that they have, despite protests to the contrary, led many to believe that these are 'rigid designators' – that they tell the exhaustive truth about God in which sign and signified are united. Intellectually, a huge number of folk recognise that these designations are metaphorical – that is, they reveal truths, they feed imagination, but they are not facts. This recognition leads some to want to lose, for example, all gendered – indeed all positive – designations of God and thereby pursue the apophatic way of God. This path – which perhaps all of us have to walk at some time – is the *via negativa* which refuses all talk of God's specific, positive qualities. In my case, finding my voice was a process of finding expansive language for God – of extending and multiplying the ways one might talk of God. For God not only is not afraid to love the different, but may be discovered in the different. And if God was in me – a trans, lesbian, disabled, chronically ill person – then she too, metaphorically, was all of these things. In asserting this metaphorical reality, which has so often been lost and ignored, God is found and freed and can set free. This 'queering' of the 'image of God' frightens so many, but God has always been bigger, freer and more capable of embracing difference than our safe human categories usually allow. If we are all bearers of the image of God, then we make fools of ourselves when we try to make that image overly determined and safe. It is a human instinct and thus understandable but when we let that instinct lead, we betray the possibilities of God which dwell within each of us.

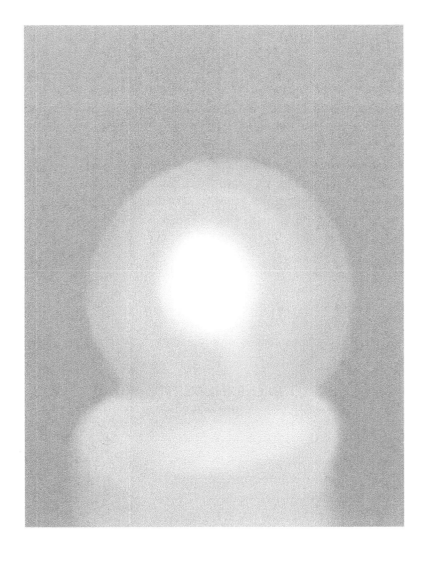

Interlude Two

I do not as a rule write 'religious' poetry. And as I have matured as a poet I've done this less and less. It is as if in being bolder in letting language have its head, I've been less willing or less able to shoehorn it into particular religious ideas. Nonetheless I wanted to include the following two early poems. It is perhaps too harsh to call them juvenilia for I hardly feel like I am a developed poet. However, they represent a stage on the way and more significantly are an attempt to play with a more expansive language for God.

She is a place[23]

she is a place
where the lost are not found
but find a joyous axis around which to spin

she is a place
where doubt arrives asylum-seeking
but receives residency right away

she is here but is yet to come
passing away yet longing to be
she is not and will not and cannot be a place
but still offers shelter on the way elsewhere

---

[3] First published in *Rain Dog* magazine, no. 11.

and sometimes she comes
an electric storm rich and bleeding
and I run like a wild horse fire-eyed terrified
of lightning and whips of rain
and then I'm caught and I'm drenched
but I'm still free still frightened

and sometimes simply in standing still
I find in her storm's eye endless passing calm
and all I may be meets everywhere and all I have been
and fractures are snapped well and fears overwhelmed
and patterns emerge like warm grain in polished oak

Creating[24]

She squats   purpling veins clogging the rivers of her legs
toes kneading   greedy for grit   for callus ground on stone
burrowing fingers into the land

And this time her making shall raise up song blue as a corpse
this time crumble night into pyres into burning into spark
and trees like cities shall pulse and roar

But brackish birthy water   nothing more comes
and grunts coiling hotter tighter softer   until dry
and her hand   a husk   lifting fists of dust

---

[24] First published in *Rain Dog* magazine, no. 11.

Seven

Beautifully Grubby Bodies

Bodies stink. Bodies sweat. Bodies decay and wrinkle. Bodies wobble. Bodies are toned, taut systems of cells. Bodies are incredible and beautiful and remarkable. Bodies hold the power to destroy themselves. And, as Janet Morley puts it, 'The bodies of grownups/come with stretchmarks and scars/faces that are lived in/relaxed breast and bellies.'[25] Bodies are the theatres of our lives.

Identity is one of the abiding themes of this book. And who we are is intimately tied to our bodily existence. Although, of course, for any number of reasons, this is extraordinarily messy and problematic. Western Christianity has not had a good track record around the body, leading many people to believe that Christians hate bodies and all their 'filthy' works. Equally, certain aspects of Western philosophical thought, influenced by Cartesianism, have been extremely corrosive when it comes to understanding ourselves as bodies. At a personal level, I have had to deal with the uncomfortable mess of living in a body that felt, for a significant proportion of my life, disconnected from how it should be. And if my experience is a relatively extreme one of what might be called 'dysmorphia', we live in a world in which an increasing number of people seem dissatisfied with the nature and shape of their bodies.

---

[25] Janet Morley, *All Desires Known* (London: SPCK 1988), p.113

The simple fact is that, from a relatively early age, I longed to change my primary sex characteristics and, in puberty, was desperate for female secondary sex characteristics. As an adult, I sought to conform my body closer to my sense of how it should be. In the popular mind the experience of male to female transsexuals is characterised by the notion of 'a woman trapped inside a man's body'. While I understand its use, I find this phrase almost entirely inadequate. For it runs the danger of equating identity with mental or psychological states – as if 'who we are' is primarily a matter of 'mind'. The problem with this way of talking is, in the very least, twofold. First, it exposes trans discourse to the countless philosophical problems generated by Cartesian-influenced mind/body distinctions – distinctions which have come under substantive attack in the past fifty years from almost all theoretical quarters (feminist, structuralist, post-structuralist etc). Sadly, there is insufficient space to grapple with this issue. And second – and, in some ways, more personally significant – the simple fact is that such talk is unfaithful to experience. For the sense of discomfort and anxiety I experienced was always located in the body. This was not a case of 'my mind' looking on at 'my body' and thinking 'I am revolted by what I see'. The profound discomfort was the result of my completely embodied existence – my thoughts were conditioned upon and lived through my bodily existence. And while I would not want to reduce my distress to a physical set of circumstances – we have hopes, dreams, anxieties and so on which are never experienced as merely measurable physical phenomena – without the reality of being a body it would make no sense.

In 2002, after years of waiting and longing and delays as a result of ill-health, I finally had sex reassignment surgery. For anyone interested in the gory details of this procedure there are countless accounts online or in print and I direct you to those. I shall only say that it is, simply because it is major surgery, bloody painful and difficult. It was also, in its way, terrifying, but ultimately the absolutely correct decision. One of the things many people don't know is that it is the job of NHS gender identity professionals to keep the choices open for trans people right up until the final surgery – for SRS really is irrevocable. Almost until the moment one is put under the anaesthetic it is possible for the trans person to say, 'No.' And I was actually grateful for that option. For I would be lying to you if I said that, even after all the years of waiting and desire, I was without doubts. Surgery is always dangerous and – even though I was reasonably well and working full-time again by the time I had it – there are any number of things which can go seriously wrong as a result of SRS including infections, urinary problems and the need for skin grafts. Equally, what if I had been a delusional idiot after all? What if, after all the conversations with psychiatrists, after my sense of becoming who I was meant to be, after my public success 'passing' as a woman, I was wrong? These were the thoughts that went through my head the night before the surgery. Only an idiot has no doubts.

The truth I discovered through SRS is that surgery doesn't change sex, it confirms it. For all practical purposes I'd already become a woman. In my head I was already a woman. As far as my family were concerned I was already a woman. The surgery genuinely mattered because it allowed me to begin to relax. It took away a huge fear of exposure. And, most of all, it enabled me to begin to enjoy my body properly. Like almost every woman in Western culture, there were and are things about my body I dislike: I'd like bigger boobs, I wish I had a prettier nose, a more shapely figure. For good or ill, that is commonly how it is to be a woman in our society – whether trans or not. But for the first time ever as a woman I could live with some bodily confidence. I was not ashamed of what lay between my legs. I was a body and it was truly good.

Christianity has often given the impression of having a huge downer on the body. St Paul's distinction between 'flesh' and 'spirit' in his Letter to the Romans is justly famous and has readily led many to equate 'flesh' with body, allowing for a dismissal of the body as corrupt, corrupting and sinful. Paul talks of God sending

his Son in 'the likeness of sinful flesh' in order to fulfil the right-
eous requirements of the Law. He goes on to suggest that,

'Those who live according to the flesh set their minds on the
things of the flesh; but those who live according to the Spirit set
their minds on the things of the Spirit. [6] To set the mind on the
flesh is death, but to set the mind on the Spirit is life and peace. [7]
For this reason the mind that is set on the flesh is hostile to God;
it does not submit to God's law. Indeed it cannot. [8] And those who
are in the flesh cannot please God.'[26]

Perhaps in these kinds of statements lie the seeds of religious
practices which have sought to find spiritual strength through
bodily mortification. And in a faith that has prioritised living 'in
the Spirit' and seeking its fruits, it is hardly surprising that many
have concluded that Christianity has a fear of the realities of
embodied existence. The treatment of women by Christianity is
also revealing about its perspective on bodies. For it has commonly been asserted that women are, through childbirth and men-
struation, more tied to bodily existence than men. Women have
readily been dismissed as 'works' of 'sinful' nature; this has been
played out in requirements for post-childbirth purification rites
and edicts against menstruating women. Mary the Mother of Jesus
has, in many traditions, been held up as the ultimate role model
for women, and yet that modelling has typically entailed de-sexing
her, leading to talk of her 'spotless womb' and even suggesting
that, in order to carry Jesus, she had to be sinless. Women have
been treated as second-class, dirty citizens of the Kingdom, and
when this attitude is added to a faith that has often over-egged a
love for Spirit, one gets close to a faith repelled by incarnation.

One obvious and sensible move when faced with such conclu-
sions is to make a distinction between 'flesh' and 'body'; that is to
say, to refuse to conflate the two notions. So, for example, when
speaking of the 'works of the flesh' in the Letter to the Galatians,

---

[26] Romans 8:5-8.

Paul mentions not only 'fornication, impurity, licentiousness ...
drunkenness, carousing' but also 'idolatry, sorcery, enmity, strife,
jealousy, anger, selfishness, dissension, party spirit, envy ...'[27]. This
latter list might equally be deemed sins of the spirit. And it is clear
that Paul, in talking about the church as the Body of Christ is not
fixated on a 'body equals bad, spirit equals good' theology. Indeed,
while one might wish to argue for inconsistencies in Paul – and
even in those letters most scholars agree originated from Paul, one
gets the sense of someone often thinking aloud rather than writing
systematic theology – I am unconvinced by any attempt to label
him a Gnostic. Nonetheless, whether grounded in his work, or a
wider cultural modesty or fear of women and nature, the church
can hardly be said to have celebrated the richness of bodily existence, especially its sexual possibilities. Certainly, by the Middle
Ages the church had codified human behaviour sufficiently to be
able to give a penance for almost every imaginable sin. From a
21st-century perspective, these 'Penitentials' make for amusing
reading. However, if they reveal the extent to which the church
wished to regulate and discipline the human body, they also reveal
that both the church authorities and the laity were extraordinarily
aware of the possibilities for pleasure on offer through our
embodied selves.

Give me bodies – wobbling, wrinkly, stretch-marked, even sur-
gically enhanced bodies. Bodies enjoying themselves. Bodies
unfrightened of their possibilities. God has no fear of bodies. This
is the truth at the heart of the incarnated God. The idea of God
emptying him- or herself into fragile flesh is one of the great shocks
of Christian theology. In so many ways it is an offence against the
other Abrahamic traditions. And it is a great affirmation of the
goodness of bodily existence – of a God who is prepared to enjoy
the company of friends at a wedding, who eats and drinks, and
who weeps at the death of a friend. And even if, theologically, we

---

[27] Galatians 5:19-21.

are inclined to take this embodied God and assert no sin on his part, we still have to deal with and embrace the implications of embodiment: physical fragility, bodily changes, living in the emotional complexity of being human. Ultimately this is defined and demonstrated in the Passion of Christ. This is a God so in love with our incarnational fragility that she seeks to redeem us through a willingness to be broken in body. A particular, embodied existence stands for all and, in her faithfulness to love, shows us the way to live.

Clearly it is possible to feel extraordinarily ambiguous about our bodies. Some people might be afraid of just quite what the strength and power of their bodies is capable of; they might be afraid of the violence that lies within them. Or others find their bodies disgusting, believing that they are too fat or too thin or that unless they work out every single day their bodies simply aren't good enough. Others will have endless surgery until they feel their bodies conform to who they really want to be.

It is easy to counsel that, in a world free of stereotypes, ruthless marketing and gender inequality, folk would be more accepting of their bodies and their possibilities. It is certainly not an entirely hopeless expectation. Nonetheless, we are so deeply inured to our cultural realities that it is difficult to gain any purchase on that claim. To claim that human wholeness or flourishing would ultimately look like complete acceptance of what God and/or nature has dealt us runs the risk of a childish fatalism. The interventions of medical science and surgery, whether in repairing congenital cleft lips or twisted limbs or in countless other remedial procedures, have improved countless lives and will continue to do so.

Nonetheless there is something significant in Christianity's prioritisation of reconciliation. Being spiritually reconciled to oneself – that is, self-acceptance – matters in our walk with God. And the question is, are there circumstances in which reconciliation cannot escape a kind of violence? In my own case I have to answer yes. There is simply no doubt that to have sex reassignment surgery is a profound act of violence against the natural body. In effect, with the help of the NHS, I took perfectly normal, functioning male genitalia and utterly destroyed and refashioned them. It was a decision that no rational, normal man would take. And though I most certainly, at a personal level, gained far more than I lost, I wiped out my manhood. It was an act of violence against the normal course of things. And yet without it I would not have achieved the degree and depth of self-reconciliation that I have. I would not have known the wholeness that comes from a real sense of self-acceptance. There is part of me that can see that life would have been easier and simpler if there had been a way in which I could have accepted my maleness and male body; but the fact is that, as painful as the surgery was, I would choose it again and again rather than be a man. Such is the strength of my gender dysphoria.

I do not think we should be afraid of the thought that there are circumstances in which reconciliation cannot avoid violence. There is a sense in which this idea lies near the heart of the Christian story. It is a kind of uncomfortable darkness. For Christ follows a path which does not turn away from violence; and that path leads to his destruction through violence. And it is only in death that Christ is raised to new life.

This, of course, is not a celebration of violence. The Cross is as much an exposure of the extent to which violence lies in the intentions and purposes of ordinary humans seeking to work for the common good; the Passion narrative is, in so many ways, an account of how ordinary people react, in the face of unselfish love, to save their familiar ways of life. But in order for that love to be faithful to God's work of reconciliation it cannot turn away from violence. It must face it, embrace it, at some level accept it and, ultimately, transform it. The resurrected Christ – the one who has been destroyed and, even in resurrection, bears the marks of crucifixion – does not walk away from the tomb on Easter morning planning revenge and violence but embodying reconciliation.

If we, as people seeking wholeness, cannot avoid the body and the violence of creation, then neither should we be afraid of the

Spirit. But we must resist over-spiritualising her. The metaphors we use for the Spirit of God are intriguing here. For the *Ruach* – the wind which hovered over creation – is in its very nature as 'wind', if indefinable, then capable of the mightiest physical effects and impact. Indeed, anyone who has ever experienced a tropical storm or hurricane will know just how physically potent wind can be. Equally, if one talks of Spirit as Breath, one immediately is drawn into physicality: for breath is, at its most basic, a bodily quality. It is a function of living, changing, fragile bodies. And then one comes to the image of the dove – the Spirit which descends upon Jesus in that form. This is a physical connection, an embodied contact. This is God's Spirit utterly caught up in physical intimacy, touching the beloved of God. These biblical images are no mere sprites or wights or ghosts. They are concrete beings which both change the life of the embodied and are caught up in the midst of embodiment. The Spirit can brace and buffet us, flow out of us, anoint us. And so the life of the Spirit should not be besmirched by trying to disconnect it from the body.

This bodily life of the Spirit is the bringing of our embodied selves to a richer and fuller expression of life. And this must be a kind of celebration and settlement with our selves, even as it is compromised by the unavoidable pressures of cultural context. For it has become clear to me that it is simply not possible to live the life of hope and celebration that God invites us to without a coming to terms with ourselves as bodily, natural creatures. Even if some folk are instinctively ascetic or attracted to asceticism, the path of denial will not do for most of us and the church serves no good purpose by encouraging it. Very few of us are carved out of the mould of John the Baptist.

The point is that if the life of the Spirit is about drawing us out into abundant life this must imply both a searching for something more and a willingness to celebrate. This abundant living must – if it is to be faithful to what is shown in the servant ministry of Christ – entail a profound willingness to live for others and to allow them to live for us; but equally it must be about reconciliation with ourselves and willingness to allow God to delight in us, as the Spirit delighted in Christ.

Often within the church we talk about the importance of abundant living and emphasise how the Holy Spirit is fundamental to it. From a Christian perspective, one will rightly want to draw a contrast between what that kind of life looks like and, in the British context in which I'm placed, some of the notorious excesses which pass for living the good life – weekend booze-ups, casual drug-taking and aspiring to the fragmented lifestyle of *Hello!*-loving celebs. Nonetheless, as someone who has perhaps more non-Christian friends than Christian ones, I am regularly struck by how very much more alive my non-Christian friends seem than many of my Christian ones. Inevitably there are exceptions on both sides, but I find this experience telling. So many Christians/churchgoers seem unwilling to embrace the vibrant and dangerous possibilities of living. There is especially in the Protestant and Reformed branches of Christianity (though not exclusively so) a puritanical strand that tends to equate abundant living with a very narrow picture of holiness. From this perspective there is a tendency to think that sanctification – growing into the likeness of Christ – is about avoiding pitfalls and sins instead of embracing life's possibilities. Abundant living is very far from just being about partying and going wild. It can equally be about discipline and asceticism, but it is never about playing it safe.

Perhaps the church needs to rediscover the medieval concept of the 'Fools' Feast'. The 'Fools' Feast' temporarily allowed the world and its comfortable values to be disrupted and inverted through excess and licensed anarchy. Young people typically took the central roles and would choose their own mock bishop or lord to act as 'Lord of Misrule'. Such wildness and parody never sat comfortably with church power and was ultimately crushed. As Charles Taylor notes[28], the reforming strand of the church, in con-

---

[28] Charles Taylor, *A Secular Age* (Cambridge: Belknap 2007), esp. Chapter 1.

cert with the secular authorities, ultimately wiped out the 'Fools' Feast'. It simply did not fit in with a church that wanted to raise the holiness of the people. And yet the notion of the 'Fools' Feast' is a symbol of the unavoidable human need for integration. An excessive emphasis upon holiness and purity simply ignores the reality of being human. The human spirit will always need to rebel against holiness as constraint. We are made for celebration, partying, excess and, frankly, the joy of being ridiculous and silly. In an ever more regulated culture, some form of 'Fools' Feast' is essential to human flourishing.

The life of the Spirit is surely about discovering possibilities of going deeper with God. Part of that process involves seeing where God might be alive and working. And that will have internal dimensions – in being prepared to recognise God in our sexual, emotional and intellectual selves and not being afraid of where that might push us – but also external ones. And in being attentive to God alive in the world, we might discover ourselves living and, crucially, embodying a more expansive life of faith than convention and tradition have classically allowed. If our life with the Spirit is a kind of dance, then it might include not only the stateliness of a waltz, but also the sexiness of a tango and the freedom of a stage dive. Blake once suggested that 'The road of excess is the path of wisdom'; God is always more active in the world than we dare imagine, for she is the constant sustainer and creator; no matter how deeply and richly we live in love we cannot exhaust or exceed her. We are pushed further out of ourselves, going beyond what we imagine we could be. Discovering more about who we truly are.

Eight

God's Call: Vocation as Violence

Surely people who want to be priests are pillocks? Wonderful, tremendously committed and often deeply loving pillocks. But pillocks nonetheless. Consider the evidence. If a person becomes ordained, then – if they work as a stipendiary – they can expect to work up to twelve-hour days and get, at best, one day off a week. They can expect to become part of an unspoken clergy culture which, even as it protests otherwise, seems to revel in the machismo of overwork and obvious busyness. Equally they can expect to be the subject of intense and, on occasions, intrusive scrutiny from congregations and neighbours fascinated by the ins and outs of their life. It's like being a celebrity for people who set their sights very low. And running alongside that is the sense in which an ordained person is simultaneously placed on an unhelpful and theologically questionable pedestal as moral exemplar while often being treated, de facto, as a mere object and a dumping ground. Some of this is chosen and appropriate – clergy, after all, make themselves available for other people's needs. Sometimes, however, it simply involves people being vile to someone they believe 'has to be nice'.

Indeed, in the role as vicar or parish priest, quite ordinary human beings are often treated in extraordinarily unpleasant ways – whether by lay people exercising petty power or by adults who, infantilised by the church and the authority of priests, behave like spoilt children. Add to this the fact that if one is a priest in the Church of England one gets to work for an organisation that is shrinking in numbers and influence. While some may argue this is a good thing, the practical, panicky effects of shrinkage can be pernicious. So, for example, paid representatives can receive the impression from those in authority that they are expected to work harder and harder to halt the decline. And if you're a woman or gay, you choose to be part of an organisation with no obvious sense of offering equal opportunities. And, for all this, you get paid relatively little for your troubles. Yes, surely one has to be a pillock to want to be a priest.

Of course, this is before one comes to what might be called the inner dimensions of priesthood – the theological shape and nature of ordained ministry – as they play off against human needs and ambitions. For it is here most of all that God undermines the foolish but oh-so-human illusions we have about ministry, exposing us to truth, cold refreshing hope and reality. These are the places where our human hunger for success meets the call to be faithful, even if that means failure.

In 2003 I was recommended for training for ordained ministry. Depending upon one's point of view, it says something about how far the church had either fallen or risen in order that it could affirm the ministry of someone like me. I think everyone – probably including the bishop – was surprised that the selectors would take such a bold step. I still take it as a sign of hope that the church can not only re-commend a trans woman for ordained ministry but then actually ordain me. There is quiet hope within the institution.

The notion of being 'called' remains one of the most curious and bewildering concepts. My sense of vocation emerged almost simultaneously with my conversion experience. Given what I've already said about how suspicious I was about my conversion, it is hardly surprising that I questioned my sense of vocation deeply. 'Feeling called', I thought, might actually be a fancy and pious way of saying that I wanted to be in charge and at the centre of things.

I have always had a suspicion that a high proportion of clergy are frustrated actors. Even if this point is moot, I am able to be honest enough with myself to admit that, from the moment I first sat in the pews, I had a hankering to lead things. But – as I see it – God actually works with our needs, gifts and desires; the key thing is to see them for what they are and not be dominated by them.

Nonetheless the notion of 'calling' suggests the idea of a voice speaking, or shouting, or even singing to us; calling us out from where we are into something else. The experience of many is a little more prosaic: it is not uncommon for those exploring vocation to feel as much cajoled or collared by clergy or friends or congregation members as 'called' by the 'still, small voice of God'. In an environment where the church is anxious for an increase in (primarily unpaid and therefore cheap) vocations to cover the massive loss of stipendiary clergy, one suspects this experience may become more common in the future. And yet the language of vocation matters and not just as a fancy rhetorical device. Words are our medium. How we talk about who we are, who God is and our relationship matters. The language of calling will resonate in different ways with different people, but crucially – in indicating the dependence of vocation upon the action of God – it articulates a profound theological reality. A reality which begins to reveal the troubling, dangerous and powerful nature of vocation.

Calling often involves language; it always, however, at some level, involves *sense*, even if we are talking about the wordless groans of our hearts. To feel called towards something suggests the pull of the external – a voice, a song, a way of life, a career – and an understanding of that pull. One feels the draw, the invite, the voice. And so we might talk of 'x' (a career, a form of action, etc) 'speaking' to us or, perhaps better, 'inviting' us. There is no need for this to involve words of course. Perhaps it is like hearing a piece of music; and we sense that somehow that tune is directed towards us, drawing us on; and we begin to respond, even if we struggle to articulate what it is we are being drawn to. But inevitably as we seek to make sense of our lives we search for words and come back again and again to the metaphor of the voice. *Vocalis* – having or finding a voice – will always be close to *vocare* – being called. And it should come as no surprise that not only is the Bible littered with God's call to individuals and communities but that words matter – as commands, as conversation, as song. And the voice which comes is often not only dangerous and insistent, but invites the listener to make absurd, questionable and sometimes terrifying responses.

Calling is about God's initiative. In the various encounters of the Bible that is the common thread. Consider Mary's encounter with Gabriel in Luke 1. Gabriel comes as a messenger of God but, given Jewish tradition, also represents the very presence of God. As such Gabriel speaks first –'Greetings, favoured one! The Lord is with you.' The text suggests that Mary is perplexed and bewildered by this greeting, perhaps even suspicious of it. It is obvious that, insofar as she is being invited to respond, she is unclear how to do so. Mary senses risk and danger and disruption in God's approach. And, however we interpret what comes next, it is clear her instinct is right: for not only is she told that she is favoured by God but that she is going to have a God-blessed son, the result of being 'overshadowed' by the power of the Holy Spirit. And yet, as she points out, she is a 'virgin' and someone who has not known a man. She may be betrothed to Joseph, but (on the basis of the language Luke uses) is quite possibly a girl who hasn't yet had her first period. What response does this child make? 'Here am I, the servant of the Lord; let it be with me according to the word.'

Feminist analyses of this encounter are well known. These have ranged from concerns over the significance of 'woman/girl' as compliant handmaid through to questions about the text as suggestive of Mary as victim of rape.[29] Even if one wishes to interrogate

---

[29] For a range of views see, e.g., Marina Warner, *Alone of All Her Sex: The Myth & Cult of the Virgin Mary* (London: Vintage 2000); Elizabeth Schussler-Fiorenza, *In Memory of Her* (London: SCM 1996); Nicola Slee, *A Book of Mary* (London: SPCK 2007) et al.

the legitimacy of feminist perspectives, there is simply no doubt that, textually, the images created by this encounter are troubling. A girl meeting God is one thing; a girl being told she will conceive a son via the 'overshadowing' power of the Holy Spirit is another. If this is God's call then it is certainly intrusive, verging on the abusive: power is massively skewed towards God and the whole scene gives the impression of a *fait accompli*. And yet the writer of Luke makes Mary's response significant. Mary's willingness to unite her will and purposes to those of God is no mere after-thought. It is, as will become clear, an echo of earlier significant biblical voices.

Even if we imagine this angelic message delivered gently, there is no obvious gentleness in it. The call seems lacking in choice; the mood is imperative – 'you will ...' The God who chooses Mary comes to her dangerously and edgily. This is not a polite or nice God, but a God of expectations. His expectations go ahead of those he comes to, as if waiting for them to catch up.

This is demonstrated in the call of Moses in Exodus. God calls to Moses out of the burning bush, but this God is no more gentle than the God who comes to Mary. In the narrative, he says, 'I will send you to Pharaoh to bring my people, the Israelites, out of Egypt.' Unlike Mary, Moses demonstrates the negotiating and wheedling skills of a grown man used to avoiding responsibility; nonetheless, God comes back at him again and again, even getting angry at Moses' unwillingness to accept his commission. God browbeats Moses into action; unlike Mary, Moses offers no verbal affirmation of his willingness to join his will to God's. His response is slightly sullen action.

God's calling of Abram is no less direct: the Lord simply speaks to Abram and tells him to leave his country and kindred. This is a command issued with a promise – a promise that Abram's heirs will be made into a great nation and a people of blessing. And Abram – man of action – obeys. He goes and steps out into the completely unknown. The tenor of First Isaiah's call is somewhat different and yet is set in a context as uncompromising as those

already mentioned. Here we find a visionary Isaiah undergoing –
in his vision – purification as painful torture. Isaiah acknowledges
that he is a man of 'unclean lips' and a seraph places a live coal
upon his lips; it is only in light of this that the call comes as a
question – 'Who shall I send? Who will go for us?' However, the
vision and the experience of the angels singing was no mere prepa-
ration for the call; they are part and parcel of it. And Isaiah unites
his will to God's in words which prefigure Mary's: 'Here am I: send
me!' Both unite their wills to that of the great 'I am'.

I have not sketched perhaps the most attractive pictures of
God's calling. This is a God presented as overpowering, terrifying,
insistent and perhaps even malicious; a God who chooses individuals and expects obedience. That is an uncompromising God,
who like an intrusive and over-confident parent presumes to know
what is best for his children and who perhaps values our response,
but expects that response to be 'Yes'.

This is a God I instinctively want to write against. I want to
pile up counter cases against this God's behaviour – emphasising
the compassion and generosity of God; the gentleness of God.[30]
And yet there is something in this picture of God I've sketched
that I want to take seriously. That both resonates in experience
and is actually worthy of serious spiritual consideration.

Firstly, it is clear that the human responses to God's call set
out in the Bible are – broadly speaking – psychologically sound.
Mary's suspicion of God's 'call' is something which I, along with
many others, know only too well. Most human experience of God
does not entail direct verbal encounter as detailed in a literary and
prophetic text like a gospel; and yet the sense of being 'drawn by
God' that I and countless others have experienced is both real and
open to question. A person who does not interrogate that sense of

---

[30] Equally, one might reasonably include quite different responses to
God's call, perhaps the classic being Jonah – symbol of those who run
away from it and discover that, ultimately, they are overtaken by God.

'call' is not taking it seriously enough. Equally, I have known many who, having felt a vocation to ordained ministry, have argued and reasoned with God, protesting their unsuitability; I have known those who like Abram have set off in obedience and those who have felt utterly unworthy and sinful. And perhaps in each of us who follow God's call there are, at different times, all of these feelings and more.

As to the picture of God suggested by the above, that is a little more difficult to deal with. As intelligent human beings informed by modern critical thought and suspicious of power narratives, we rightly want to interrogate this picture of God and many will want to reject it. But I want to say this: that though I am critical of anything that might legitimise rape or torture, metaphoric or not, in the name of God, there are dimensions of authenticity in this alien God. This is no domesticated, easy God; this is almost certainly not the kind of God that one would invent for one's own comfort. This God is neither a comfort blanket nor a consumer accessory adopted in order to make one's life feel complete. In an age in which the God who is often preached is one who is friendly, not overly demanding and gentle, this is a God who is alien and strange. And, yet, faithful. This is no Hellenic God, full of bewildering, yet very human, caprice. This is no God who comes to us as a wise old man appearing out of nowhere on a desolate road with a bewitching offer to make all our dreams come true; whose offers are never quite what they seem.

In Scorsese's *The Last Temptation of Christ*, Jesus' opening line is 'God loves me. I know God loves me. I wish he'd stop.' There is something of this in the kind of God I have been discussing. This is the God who calls but who pushes us out so very far from our ordinary human desires and expectations. This is the God who drives Jesus out into the wilderness, who expects Jesus' followers to take up the Cross and follow him and who leads Jesus on that bleak road to Jerusalem. This is the God who fills Mary's heart full of rejoicing and yet gifts her a son who pierces her heart. This is the God who is with Moses and yet is behind mass slaughter, who pushes his chosen people out into the wilderness for countless years, who blesses Moses greatly and yet doesn't allow him to enter the Promised Land. And somewhere in all this bleakness, in this wilderness and so much night, is the mystery of Love.

One of the reasons 'calling' matters is that it indicates a way of being that resists certain modern pictures of human living and identity. These pictures are inclined to view us as individualised economic units whose main work is to maintain a reasonable level of existence for ourselves and ensure that we are not too great a burden on a society comprised of individuals who come together merely for mutual benefit. In this context, what matters most is not who we are, what gifts we have and to what we are drawn but having a job. A society ordered on this kind of principle will be more concerned about how its citizens can be useful than in helping them discern what they are really about. The purpose of education will entail encouraging young people to pursue paths that are effective, successful and productive rather than seeking to help them figure out who they are, be attentive to what they are drawn to and discern what they are capable of.

For calling is – even if it understood in a secular way, demythologised from God – about being drawn out of oneself towards something: a career, a life, a way of going on. And so it is also about *response*. It requires commitment, a joining of one's will to something other. It is about a 'yes' and then giving of ourselves to that direction. And it is never passive. Indeed, sometimes the grace is in the fighting. For if God comes to us as one intent on gouging our eyes out, what else is one to do? In the Book of Genesis, God famously wrestles with Jacob. Neither Jacob nor God are messing about. As Michael Symmons Roberts has Jacob put it:

His fist smashes my face.
That's no wrestler's move;
so it's bare knuckles now. Okay.

There's blood in my eye,

the lid swells to a hood.
I use my head and butt him.[31]

God pops Jacob's hip out to take him down, but Jacob will not yield; he demands a blessing and receives one before letting God go. Travelling with God, then – the way of vocation – is never merely about a job or even a course of action. It is about the shape and direction of a life and accepting the prospect that this may change us, for either good or ill. We might even get bloody, but within it may lurk true blessing. And if we are not merely working at jobs – even though sometimes, in order to protect ourselves and survive, we must think that way – we are following a way of life. It is not lifestyle, that great modern idea of what life our jobs may allow us to lead, but living. And if God is the true ground of our being and the very heart of what we most truly are, her call will always be the primary one; when she comes calling, we may resist, be suspicious and so on, but we can be assured we are being drawn out into our deepest, truest selves.

If ordained ministry is about living, then those who embody it must simply accept that they are exposing themselves to the very heart of life: the fragility of existence, the ups and downs of external circumstance, the possibility of joy rather than pleasure and the terrifying love of God. For ordained ministry as vocation is the opposite of life seen as a mere job – a job which enables one to have enough money to make life bearable and pleasurable, to ensure a comfortable old age and be a useful member of an institution, community or society. Ordained ministry is one way of walking into our true selves, for it is about living the world aright. And this is not a moral matter; it is not about behaving according to this rule or that (even though the ordained are often shoe-horned into that picture); it is about seeking to live on grace, trust in God and be unafraid to be exposed to and stand up for the real

---

[31] Michael Symmons Roberts, *Corpus* (Cape: London, 2006)

and apparently impossible nature of the world – that though the world is cruel, unfair and often vile, love still lies at its centre and will yet transform it.

Ordained ministry, then, is one way in which we may respond to Jesus' claim that 'those who seek to save their life will lose it, but those who lose their life for my sake will gain it'. In being prepared to respond to the call of God, we let go of one picture of ourselves and the world, but actually receive in return something more remarkable: an invitation to become who we really are. Clearly, ordained vocation is a secondary calling, for the primary call is the Christian one – the call to live our true humanity by nothing more or less than living for others and for God. But for some of us, the shape of that way of living – the method by which we will expose ourselves to reality – will be ordained ministry. And it will be the way God cherishes us.

But we should not become over-romantic and indeed over-theological in our assessment of the reality of ordination. For in being ordained we are most definitely responding to God but also jumping into bed with an institution. I have already indicated the extent to which I take the willingness of the church to ordain me as a sign of hope. And yet I cannot deny the silencing which ordained ministry entails. That is to say, it is right that ordained ministry is understood as a kind of sacrifice – for, in being ordained, we are seeking to let go of our natural instinct to be in control and let God lead and hold us. But are there edges to that sacrifice? Are there places where the expectations of the church, perhaps even of God, should not be allowed to transgress? When I was ordained I was in a very committed and loving relationship with another woman, which had lasted for a significant number of years. I had followed sensible advice from ordained friends to keep my mouth shut about this relationship during both selection and training and when I got ordained. 'Be pragmatic,' I was told. 'The church has got itself totally screwed up about sexuality, especially the sexuality of the ordained, and if you want to follow your vocation, keep quiet.' It was a sensible voice. It was the voice used to playing the game. It was the voice that didn't want to upset the institution. It was the voice of silence.

We are all compromised. We are people of unclean hands and lips. We make bargains with ourselves and others to get things done. I have to accept that I made a choice in order to follow my sense of call. I was discreet about who I was as a lesbian and about my relationship – a relationship of serious length and commitment. And my partner was complicit in and supportive of that choice. I accept responsibility for my decision. And yet I cannot deny the structural sin and injustice of a system which, out of fear, prejudice and an uncharitable reading of scripture, expects silence from significant numbers of its servants. And I cannot, at least at an emotional level, escape the feeling that the price of keeping silent, of playing the game, was the ultimate break up of that relationship. Yes, there were other factors, not least my selfishness. But in the end a long relationship got lost amidst the public demands of ministry.

One – not unreasonable – response is to say, 'You knew what the institution was like; live with it and your choices.' Perhaps that is what is required from those of us whose lives do not readily fit into the limited ambitions and visions of the institution and yet sense that following the call of God leads them to try to live with it. But there is a deep tension here and a reminder of the costliness of God's call to life.

God's call to a life of love clearly should not be limited to and equated with being within the church. Down that path lies a kind of idolisation of the church and a reductive conception of the nature of the Kingdom. Nonetheless, for all its idiocy and flaws, I remain convinced that the church is a place of grace. At the very least there are very many remarkable people associated with it who are prepared to put themselves on the line for the sake of greater peace and justice in the world; there are equally so many within the church committed to ways of spiritual being which offer profound critiques of consumerist and utilitarian conceptions of humanity. There are just too many people seeking to follow the way of Jesus, often in trying circumstances, for grace to be deniable. And so being faithful to the call of love can involve service within the church, even as it seeks to encourage greater commitment to the wider Kingdom.

But any church must reflect its participants – their flaws, prejudices and sinfulness. And this will also be reflected at a structural level. And should any of this be an apology for beastliness, for institutional silencing and for a refusal to grow? Of course not. But reality has to be acknowledged and faced and negotiated. And the road to the Promised Land is long and sometimes bleak, and there is no guarantee that any of us will get to walk upon it. This is the kind of situation many of us are called to minister within. It isn't easy and sometimes it does not feel very hopeful. One is often left asking what kind of God calls the likes of me to give themselves to the kind of hopelessly bewildered, sometimes warring and often angry place that is the church.

To put it another way: there is getting lost and then there is getting lost. Ordination is indeed one of the ways in which we may lose our life for Christ's sake and receive it back afresh. But one of its attendant dangers is the way in which the expectations of congregations and the institution itself and, sadly, one's own fears can lead to the loss of dimensions that sustain us. Ordained ministry is one of the ways in which those of us called to it reveal or expose our true selves to the world. The dog collar is not necessarily fancy dress. But the experience of many gay people (and no doubt of many others) within ministry is of being expected to wear a mask – for the sake of not upsetting a very noisy minority of those who seem threatened by gay people. And one of the dangers of wearing a mask for too long is that you forget who you were beneath it. There are many kinds of silencing and many forms of mask that those who are ordained may have to deal with in their ministry; to be expected to bear the silence and wear the mask, for the sake of making life for the institution easier and simpler, will always rank among the least attractive dimensions of church.

As explored in other parts of this book, it is clear that the

Living God is a God who strips away illusion, rubbish and trickery. It is right and proper that those who are ordained experience a sense of commissioning and affirmation and delight in ordination. But I sometimes wonder if this is another one of God's easy faces, provided to get us up and running. And behind that is a deeper call. And that call is actually to faithfulness.

When I was first ordained I thought I was going be God's gift to the church; I thought I was going to be such a success and make such an impact. I imagined my gifts and talents, at the service of God, would be transformative – would somehow reach out to the broken and the disappointed, encouraging people to come to church and so on. I felt so full of energy and so built up. However, it is not success that one is called to, but faithfulness. My own ministry has been dogged by illness, to the point where I have on occasion been left questioning whether it is sustainable. And partly as a result of an illness that has regularly left me unable to be, in conventional secular terms, 'dynamic' and 'successful', and partly because of the fragmentary nature of parish ministry, in which pastoral, administrative and managerial demands pull in different directions, I have often felt like a failure. But the call remains: to proclaim that the world is shaped by love and redeemed by love despite so much that insists otherwise. And how much more difficult this is to do when one has scant evidence of success and achievement and power and one feels like a failure. And, though it tastes like bitter herbs on the tongue, for this stripping away I am sometimes thankful.

Perhaps, then, the ordained are ultimately called to be artists – to be poets. Wallace Stevens once suggested that 'poets are the priests of the invisible'.[32] It is intriguing to alter this formulation to 'priests are the poets of the invisible'. Part of this way of living will be a kind of attentiveness to and openness to the Living God.

---

[32] Wallace Stevens. *Opus Posthumous*. New York: Alfred A. Knopf, 1957. p.169

Part of the artist's gift is attention to the world, but also a capacity to shape it in such ways that possibilities are opened up for others. Priesthood is about exposure to reality, perhaps even about being knocked down by that reality. And yet there is this call to faithfulness: not only to proclaim Love in the face of failure, but to open up ways for others to encounter it.

And so the ordained must not be afraid of the startling nature of the Living God – the way in which she exceeds our formulations and attempts at making her in our own image. For the Love she offers is not on our terms, but on hers. And that can entail the breaking down of our comfortable ways of going on. And in order to survive this and not fall back into cosy formulas once again, perhaps we will need the courage of an artist: an ability to face reality as it is and yet, in partnership with God, to help shape new imaginative possibilities. Sometimes this task of opening consciousness will involve remaking language and imagery; and sometimes it will entail reminding ourselves and others of the deep hope found in what we already have. For some – poets like me – this will involve specific acts of writing and creation in the Scottish 'Makar' sense; for most, it will be a way of living in the world – liveliness to the possibilities and power of language[33], an openness to the transcendent and so on.

What kind of God would call people into a ministry that leaves them stripped and compromised, perhaps even to the point where they feel they have lost what really matters to themselves? Probably not a good God. Probably not one we would invent for ourselves or want to follow. Most of us would want to say that God is not so cruel. That God is about calling us into life and truth. And this is correct. But this life is so very far from being safe and insulated. To be exposed to the fullness of life is to be exposed to its fragility and to come face to face with compromise and uncontrolled circumstance.

---

[33] Whether those words be old and already minted, like the Book of Common Prayer, or virgin and fresh.

This will mean no safety from brokenness – our own, that of others and, of course, of institutions, especially those we work for. And this brokenness, if we take it seriously and will not hide from it, may exact a terrible cost upon us.

Surely you have to be a pillock to be a priest. But God has always used pillocks and fools. Who else would be stupid enough to open their hearts to the world and find love therein?

Nine

Blasphemy as Prayer

How far do we have to fall before we start to think that the crucified and forsaken God is not enough? Where do we go when the
broken God dies? What do we cling to when we are left living
among the fragments of a story that once made sense?

Only a fool would deny that chronic illness is corrosive and
vile. I have already spoken about my early experiences of Crohn's
Disease. Of how I felt stripped. Of how a picture I had of myself
– as lively, energetic, young – began to die and along with it one
kind of image of God. I have spoken about resurrection – about
the discovery of the fullness of the suffering, broken God and the
life that comes through embracing her. I want now to go further.
And possibly deeper. I want to explore what kind of God and what
kind of hope might be possible in the midst of progressive, aggres-
sive disease when one feels truly pushed beyond the limits. And I
want to examine what kind of prayer might be possible in that
place. For although I have been blessed with periods when my
health has improved and my Crohn's has effectively been dormant,
my life has generally been a slow erosion of strength and often a
feast of pain. Since that initial two-year period, I have been in hospital as an emergency countless times, been close to death through
blood poisoning, spent months at a time unable to eat solid food
and have had large sections of bowel removed. I have ended up
clinically depressed and have struggled, on far too many occasions, to exercise anything resembling what most people would

consider 'full-time Christian ministry'. I have been on numerous different medications, including some which have had side-effects similar to the symptoms of the actual disease, and have spent more time in hospital than your average medical professional. There have been too many occasions when I have effectively felt too tired and stripped out to hope.

What does it mean to be a person of hope not only in the midst of awful, pointless pain, but in the midst of suffering with no apparent end in sight? Let me be clear: I am not especially interested here in whether or not suffering/pain can ever be justified. Nor am I especially concerned with whether God 'inflicts' pain upon humans (although such a notion is abhorrent to me). Rather, I am interested in what 'hope' might be said to look or feel like in situations which not only feel hopeless, but also which many sensible people might suggest *are* hopeless. Illness can be one of those situations, although there are, of course, many others. And surely exploring what hope looks like in such situations is no mere academic matter – it is both a live personal issue for me and for many others and, surely, something that is of huge importance for Christians. For we see ourselves as people of hope – indeed, our faith might be said to be founded on hope: the hope offered by the crucified and resurrected Christ. If that hope cannot speak into all situations, including extreme ones like desperate ill-health, then it's neither use nor ornament.

Perhaps the starting point should be the Christian hope of eternal life: for surely the deepest Christian hope is our own resurrection in Christ. This hope itself is founded on our faith that Jesus Christ himself was resurrected from the dead. According to this picture, Christian hope – especially for those for whom this life is a vale of tears – lies only beyond this life in the next. But surely this notion is appalling. Am I over-reacting? I don't think so. Firstly, such a picture of hope says to those who suffer, 'Just put up with it and you'll get your reward later.' It seems to accept, in an uncreative way, the injustice of reality. Equally, to claim that Christian hope lies beyond this life is really to say that Christian hope doesn't speak into this life except as something to be hung on for. I think I know what it is to hang on to hope by a very thin thread, but surely hope is more than just a promise of what is to come? The way in which St John talks about 'eternal life' suggests that such a view of hope is inadequate. For although he clearly has a sense of the life to come, he also strongly indicates that eternal life – the life of hope – is breaking into and available in this life: in passages like John 6:54, which claims, 'Those who eat my flesh and drink my blood have eternal life.'

Furthermore, the resurrection of Jesus Christ isn't simply a first fruit of the life to come, but (to borrow T.S. Eliot) 'the still point of the turning world'. That is to say, it isn't just some deeply impressive conjuring trick which proves that God cannot be defeated by death, but the fundamental perspective from which the whole world should be judged. God is saying, in effect, that though the world may give the appearance of being nothing more than painful, violent, or directed by self-centred human concerns, that is not how it is in its full reality. In reality, at its heart is hope revealed and confirmed in the resurrection of Christ. And this is not just hope for the next life, but hope for this world we are living in now – that can be claimed and lived in the face of everything speaking against it.

The question is what that means here and now. Living in hope, at its most basic, is seeking to live on God's promises. It is, then, a kind of commitment or action, constantly reaffirmed. Part of living on those promises is taking Jesus' resurrection seriously – that is, using it as the starting point for seeing the world aright. God's hopefulness is seeking to break into the world, to transform it: to take appalling situations, like painful chronic illness, and say, 'The Living God may yet be discovered here.' In earlier chapters I've tried to indicate ways in which that is true but which also demonstrate that seeking to live on God's promises does not mean that life becomes simply unalloyed joy and wonder. Indeed, if that happened one might rightly be suspicious that one was living out a fantasy. Illness is very real and even if one is cured, it leaves its marks, especially in the case of serious illness. Rather, Christian hope in appalling situations often has the character of 'holding on' and of resistance; it involves discovering sufficient hope in God to avoid falling into despair. Sometimes, hope has the character of simply setting one's face against despair.

My early experience of chronic illness was very much that of discovering the suffering or forsaken God, and the extent to which I have encountered resurrection has been grounded in crucifixion. But as I have travelled further into the corrosive reality of such illness, it is as if I've found less and less purchase on that suffering God. It is as if illness has broken even him. Or if that seems simply too heretical and unorthodox, try this: it is as if, in illness, the suffering God reveals a new dimension in the darkness. This is the God utterly hidden from ordinary life. This is the God only found in the fragments of ourselves and our hopes and dreams. This is 'the hidden God'.

There is a place beyond 'holding on' and resistance where we are actually unable to take any more pain and suffering and, in effect, we let go of the thin thread of hope we have left. It is a place very close to despair. I have been there. In 2007/8 I went for nearly a year without ordinary food, and every single day was pain, and depression almost swallowed me whole. I have been there in the past year when my bowels seemed to go mad again, when food became synonymous with discomfort and pain, and when, in the aftermath of a relationship of twelve years, I thought I was going insane. It is in that place, however, that I have encountered God at her most startling. In saying this I recognise that I risk simply restating a familiar cliché of faith – that it is at one's lowest that one discovers God's surprising and odd power. And this is indeed a common experience and the ubiquity of that experience is the reason for the cliché. However, experience not only demands that I say it, but also – more interestingly – that I outline just how peculiar that encounter was. For this is God at her most intimate – the one who simply *is* when all else seems lost. This is God beyond doctrine and without boundaries. This is God beyond reason and the uses we would make of her. Let me put it like this.

This is the God who refutes the claim of the non-religious that belief in God is just a kind of crutch. For the God who comes to us in such broken places is anything but a crutch. We cannot use her: she comes in her own time and meets us when we have nothing else left. And all she is is Love. She is not comfort, but the thinnest thread holding you above despair. This is not a God we can summon up for ourselves and for our own purposes. The medieval mystic Meister Eckhart said, 'To use God is to kill him.' Well, in some respects we only truly discover this in the utmost point of our need when all hope seems to have faded: for in such places we cannot use God for our own ends (to make our life better or more hopeful), but simply have to wait for her to come. And this is why she is 'hidden': she only becomes available as gift. She cannot be willed into being; she is not present even in the ordinary run of life's ups and downs. She is hidden from us until we are seemingly utterly broken. This is God in all her stark love – stripped of sentiment and our manipulations; the God who holds crucifixion and death in her depths.

Perhaps it is in such a place that one most truly learns how to pray. The Great War poet Wilfred Owen once suggested, 'I have heard cadences of harps not audible to Sankey, but which were strung by God ... there is a point where prayer is indistinguishable from blasphemy. There is also a point where blasphemy is indistinguishable from prayer.'[34] The context for Owen's remark was of course the butchery of the trenches; in it he was trying to capture how his experience contrasted so startlingly with his conventional Evangelical upbringing. But there is something remarkably accurate and holy in his understanding of prayer in the darkness and in conditions of abridged hope. There are so many things that rapacious chronic illness/pain does not hold in common with war, but they are both places where prayer is practised *in extremis*. They are both circumstances in which words can be as empty and ceremonial

---

[34] Harold Owen & John Bell, *Wilfred Owen: Collected Letters* (Oxford: OUP 1967), p.534

as the Cenotaph on Whitehall; in which the only proper prayer is an animal cry, a groan aimed wildly towards heaven. Beyond the wordless cry, what words will suffice for prayer under extreme conditions? And can prayer properly be spoken there?

In times of anxiety and pain, I know many have found the Psalms enormously comforting, but they have rarely helped me in the midst of really active pain, fear or crisis – that is, in the very moment when I've been assaulted by the pain my chronic ill-health has sometimes thrown at me. Under such circumstances, I've needed something blunter. Siegfried Sassoon's poem 'Attack!' closes with the line, 'O Jesus, make it stop!' Those words (with the addition of suitable expletives) are much nearer to the kind of language substantial enough to take the weight of prayer. Perhaps these have been the words of countless people down the centuries caught in situations of intense need, where our usual pious formulations seem as adequate as the promises of a tyrant. Sassoon wrote those words as the closing line of a poem about a trench attack in a now ancient war, the Great War; yet because they were generated out of experience *in extremis*, they retain the power and substance to speak into human extremes. I do not think that it's cheap to say that one does not have to have experienced being shelled on the Western Front, or in Bosnia, Afghanistan or the Lebanon, to know times when, as Sassoon's poem also states, 'hope, with furtive eyes and grappling fists, flounders in mud' and the only prayerful Christian response is 'O Jesus, make it stop!'

When Owen claims 'there is a point where prayer is indistinguishable from blasphemy. There is also a point where blasphemy is indistinguishable from prayer' he is suggesting that in some extreme circumstances the sacred and profane meet and embrace. This embrace is often a wordless cry. 'O Jesus, make it stop!' gives some words for that cry. Its direct, terse nature makes it almost an expletive, a prayerful 'f-word'. Indeed, the 'O Jesus' has both the feel of a petition and the edge of the modern usage heard every day on our streets as a throwaway expletive. To try to offer to God anything more nuanced in times of abject pain, terror or fear, I sense would be an attempt to soften reality. The dreadfulness of pain and the dignity of the sufferer demand words as immediate and as fierce as Sassoon gives us.

Sometimes the only suitable prayer is blasphemy; we dishonour God and reality if we do not offer up words of blasphemy and cursing. For, although the Psalms and the patterns of our conventional prayers can bring comfort and encouragement, indeed speak deeply into our need, there are places beyond comfort. There are places that are both tragedy and utter barrenness, and perhaps can only be appropriately experienced as such. The philosopher Gillian Rose famously used Staretz Silouan's 'Keep your mind in hell and do not despair' as the epigraph for her autobiography.[35] This phrase underlined Rose's determination to look reality in the eye, especially as she faced death from cancer. She was determined not to take flight into a comforting vision of wholeness any more than she was prepared to be reduced to bitter atomistic selfishness by her disease. Her commitment was a profound statement on God's invitation to become our true selves.

For as Christians – as those who proclaim God's hope and seek to live on – we run the endless risk of trying to live 'outside' reality. When we face situations where hope is actively cut short, where barrenness is reality, we may seek to take flight into comfort and illusion. We may pretend that God is testing us and we may try to take the edge off the pain and destruction we face by painting it better than it really is. However, sometimes things genuinely have turned to shit. Equally we may be tempted to fall into bitter selfishness; we may be consumed body and soul by the world and we may, quite understandably, become vile. But I remain convinced that the Christian vocation is to remain clear-eyed and clear-hearted. To simply keep walking into the desert. To wait on the God who comes towards us in the darkness.

This may seem absurdly bleak. For in what, then, does the

---

[35] Gillian Rose, *Love's Work* (London: Chatto & Windus 1995)

hope consist? The hope consists in God and God alone. Sam Wells once called the Christian story 'a satire on the story that there is no story'[36]; Christians will not ultimately end the story in barrenness, failure and tragedy. We will want to say that even if the world is experienced as a human tragedy it is ultimately a divine comedy. But still we are called to be faithful to experience and reality; clear-eyed and honest. Although we may each experience many kinds of resurrection and love, there are dimensions of living which should be seen and lived for what they are. And the hope of God in those places is not about trying to find ways of 'feeling better' about them, but is about waiting. And that waiting may take till the end of time to be brought to fullness. How we live in the midst of a world which seemingly lacks grace does matter. For in participating in the practices of Confession and Forgiveness, of Eucharist and so on, we hint at a story which exposes the emptiness of a story-less world.

And if – as seekers after our true selves - we are left waiting upon God, maybe the ultimate prayer is silence. This is, perhaps, the most difficult face of the dark God. For as human beings, and especially when one feels called to write, we rightly consider language to be our medium. We are awash with words – so much so, perhaps, that many of us no longer trust them. They are used for such unscrupulous, utilitarian ends – whether to convince us to believe a politician's dodgy story or to get us to buy a particular brand of washing powder. Words so often do not seem to be what they really mean and so we multiply them as if hoping we shall find some sense. Perhaps because, as Barbara Brown Taylor once suggested, they do not nourish us.[37] We are caught in an ironic 'famine' of words: for there is an abundance of them, but they contain no nourishment. Our words look so good but they turn to dust in our mouths. But to wait is to shut up. That is one reason

---

36 Sam Wells, *Transforming Fate into Destiny* (Carlisle: Paternoster Press 1998), p.171

why it is so difficult. And as the Desert Fathers and Mothers knew only too well, it is when the devil comes to tempt and taunt us. But only silence – the dark silence of God, pregnant with new things – will ultimately do.

Perhaps the sheer difficulty of silence indicates that it is one of our deepest vocations. For this is not just stillness, nor is it the mere absence of babble. It is simply being in the presence of God, stripped of all illusion and distraction. And, in so many ways, this vocation is difficult for us. For not only are many of us caught up in a nexus of distraction almost every moment of the day, but, more significantly, we struggle extremely hard to deny ourselves sufficiently to let God in. And as one of those who has known the degrading, sinful effects of silencing (that is, of being silenced), I am so resistant to silence – even the holy silence of the dark, Living God. For though I know her call is not about destroying me or eroding my sense of self, it is still about a kind of annihilation. And when you have struggled long and hard to be yourself, even when you know that God's Way of letting go is life, it is almost impossible to plunge into her beautiful darkness. Perhaps all one can do is jump. And trust that the waters will at least be warm as you sink down into the depths.

---

[37] Barbara Brown Taylor, *When God is Silent* (Boston: Cowley 1998)

Interlude Three

Is it absurd to try to articulate silence? Probably. And just as an overdose of sincerity makes for bad poetry, so does too much abstraction and airy metaphysics. Nonetheless, the experience of being pushed to the edge of hope and prayer has been the ground of some of my poetry. Here are two attempts to speak out of the place of silence.

The Risen Life[38]

You wake to a sting between the shoulder blades,
as if someone's folded a crease down your back.
The silence hurts, and the light unexpected –
grey, not quite morning, glowing at the edges
as if electric is involved. So many people,
lying down, confined, each in their own bay
the slow heave of chests, a faint scent (antiseptic perhaps?)
the calm.

Not remembering for a second what has happened to you,
then feeling out from the inside a kind of shock
shivering down through your forehead, teeth, neck

---

[38] First published in *Smiths Knoll* magazine no 42

a fear about what might have been removed.

There is a nurse, she could be a nurse, someone who smiles
who is not afraid of wounds, whose eyes twinkle
as she holds a finger to her mouth
when you begin to speak.

Silence[39]
(*For D.S.*)

As when Eadfrith crunched onto the holy shore
kicked the sting of the sea from between his toes
quaked beneath the vault of heaven
and understood.

How he traced the shapes of *Alpha* and *Omega*
on the palms of his unpromising hands
asked to bear the blessing
prayed the ink would stir the Word uncurl
blink itself awake.

We too have known that startling silence of the heart
the world's refusal to speak.
We too have come to that wide unyielding desert
the wilderness which steals.

Too late we ask to receive. Too easily we hide.
Too late we understand: no pilgrim may be given more.

---

[39] First published in *Third Way* magazine, Vol 33, number 3, April 2010

Ten

The God of The Other

Perhaps the ultimate call upon human beings is to reconciliation. For surely the fundamental point of the resurrection of Jesus Christ is forgiveness. The resurrection is the defining moment for creation because it is the final demonstration of God's love for us. And the nature of that love is 'You are forgiven'. What is being offered to each and every one of us is a chance to live as the reconciled; to make reconciliation our very way of going on. This clearly has implications across every aspect of life – international, national, local and personal. The Way of Christ is an invitation to love our enemies, to bring an end to oppositions of mistrust, fear and sometimes hate, between Gentile and Jew, male and female and so on.

And so this resurrection God is the God of 'The Other' or the Stranger. That is to say, the God who is not afraid of difference, of the alien, of the strange and of otherness; who takes all that is seen as 'other' and frightening and alien and reconciles it to herself. This is the God who, for our sake, allows herself to become our scapegoat and perceived enemy – the ultimate 'Other' – and redeems our fear and hate. This is the God who, from the first, comes to us as the ultimate stranger: for Christ comes as the emptying of God's unsullied love into the world and invites us to make a faithful response. This invitation takes the form of dethroning ourselves from the centre of living: to 'deny ourselves and take up the Cross' and live reconciled to God. When Christ takes this message to the heart of his world – Jerusalem – the invitation is definitively rejected. And, in the face of death and through death,

Christ continues to confront us with the way of forgiveness and reconciliation that is love.

As soon as one begins to reflect upon 'self' and 'identity', the notion of 'The Other' becomes striking, potent and perhaps undeniable. It seems clear to me that, even if one is suspicious of psychological concepts, the idea of 'The Other' resonates powerfully in human experience. Perhaps the most familiar examples lie in what might be called 'external targets'. This especially happens during wartime when nations feel they are in life-or-death struggles for ideas and the upper moral ground and have to convince their populaces of the need to fight. So, for example, in World War Two, one finds the most extraordinary demonisation and stereotyping used on both sides to characterise the opponent as 'The Other'. The Japanese were characterised simultaneously as primitive and bestial, yet cunning, rapacious and dangerous; as morally questionable and yet possessed of their own insane zeal. What is intriguing is how quickly this picture was put away by the American administration after the war and yet how in the '80s, when Americans felt under threat from Japanese industry, this vision of 'The Other' became popular again.[40]

The notion of 'The Other' takes a similar pattern in diverse situations, no matter to whom it is applied. History is littered with examples of racism, sexism, misogyny, class fear and homo- and transphobia in which various groups – on the basis of skin colour, race, gender, sexuality etc – have been readily turned into 'The Other' by the dominant and normative power group. And the patterns of dismissal are, sadly, all too typical: inferiority is asserted and yet the target group is often seen as devilishly cunning or possessing some animal skill that threatens civilisation. In the case of anti-semitism, Jews are simultaneously seen as sub-human and yet rapaciously skilled at manipulation; in the case of misogyny,

---

[40] For a compelling examination of this, see J Dower, *War Without Mercy* (London: Faber 1986)

women have been categorised as capricious, soft, tied to nature and emotionally unstable and yet full of wiles with which to entrap men. This creation of 'The Other' is simultaneously crude – for it relies on cheap, false stereotypes – and yet curiously compelling – for it appeals to a deep human need to belong, to feel safe, and to be part of a successful, powerful group.

I am intrigued by how the notion of 'The Other' plays out within our own selves. As an internal concept 'The Other' refers to those aspects and dimensions of our selves we readily write off, are afraid of or wish to bury or destroy. These are the things within ourselves we perceive as having cunning, dangerous powers but which we demonise and want to wipe out or ignore. Even though many will be suspicious of this kind of talk, it is not necessary to posit the existence of something like 'the Id' in order to appreciate the kind of fear and anxiety some feel about aspects of themselves or persistent thoughts or desires. Historically, when society was more prejudiced and had sanctions against it, being gay was an experience many treated as an internal 'Other' to be buried and afraid of, but it was hugely powerful. In my teen years, there was simply no doubt that my desire to be a girl was precisely the kind of dimension of myself that I wanted to wipe away, and tried to bury and destroy. No matter what strategy I adopted it seemed to come back stronger and more cunning. It was a part of me that sickened me because it seemed abnormal, other, and made me different. It was 'wrong' and needed be excised so that I could fit in.

The journey into womanhood was a journey into reconciliation. In embracing The Other within I have become more myself and have come to know the God of the Stranger who brings reconciliation and therefore hope. But there is always a shadow. As I've suggested elsewhere, the God of Reconciliation is always working in the shade. Indeed she typically works in the dark, among the apparently dead, among the discarded, in the darkness at the foot of the cross. What if reconciliation goes deeper than merely accepting myself as a woman, as a lesbian and so on? What if it means re-embracing and loving that within me that once was male? What if

I have simply tried to make all that I once considered 'male' or 'mannish' into a new Other? That is, into something that is frightening and threatening and always in danger of subverting my carefully constructed life. In this picture, the Other becomes a shadow in the background that might make my life difficult and might lead to my being singled out as a 'freak' or unacceptable. This worry feels both absurd and yet curiously real. Sometimes, when I spend a considerable amount of time in the company of cis-women[41] I become conscious of certain ways I have of talking and behaving – ways that strike me not simply as 'mannish' or 'tomboyish' but actually 'blokey'. These things are very hard to pin down and feel almost indefinable, but still they are there. And – given how successful I've become at passing as a cis-woman – I don't want them to 'out' me. If I want to tell someone I'm trans, I want to do it on my terms and in my time. But sometimes I fear there is blokeishness within me threatening to out me unexpectedly.

To open up to those aspects of myself that I consider 'male' or 'mannish' has been akin to walking among the dead. It has been a journey into so many things I'd rather forget. It has been a walk into darkness. It has been like the work of a cold case pathologist – someone who searches for long-dead bodies carefully hidden in unexpected places and then disinters and dismantles them, trying to unlock their secrets.

Perhaps most of us would prefer, for the sake of avoiding cringing embarrassment, to forget the way we were as a gauche child or teenager. This is inevitably amplified when one feels one was living the wrong sex. But the more I have tried to go back into my story, the extent to which I have suppressed memories and details has become increasingly striking. As an adult I've always claimed this was the result of taking vast quantities of psycho-

---

[41] 'Cis-woman', as a gender theory term, has its origin in the Latin-derived prefix *cis*, meaning 'to the near side'. In this case, 'cis' refers to the alignment of gender identity with assigned gender.

tropic drugs as an undergraduate – and perhaps there's some truth in that – but my fear is that part of my subconscious has suppressed difficult details. And the most difficult thing for me to face – from the point of view of who I am now – was that I was so very male as a boy. I was such a typical boy.

Here is what I loved: I loved toy guns. I mean I absolutely adored them. I had piles of the things and my single favourite game was 'war'. And I was good at it – I was a natural leader and 'general'. I could get people to do things for me. I loved the theatre of hiding in the long grass, appearing suddenly to 'kill' someone, making them count to ten as the condition of resurrection. And in my head I was one of those great heroes of British war films – whether the wounded man who gets left behind to take out the enemy in a last-ditch effort or the hero running into the lion's mouth for Queen and Country. I loved films like *Dunkirk* and *The Dambusters* and any tale of male derring-do. And when my mates and I weren't refighting WW2 we were on our bikes, holding mini-race meetings and pretending we were 'grass track' stars – because as a child they were my heroes. Most weekends my dad would take my brother and me off to see the champions of the day – Gerald Short, Chris Baybutt and Simon Wigg – battle it out on 500cc death machines in a field. Being on a bike was one of my natural homes. I could pull a wheelie and hold it the whole length of the village green – fifty metres at least. Indeed, there was surely part of me born to be on two wheels, for I was also a childhood motorbike champion, hurtling around a grass track in imitation of my heroes, taking mad tumbles and going for glory until, at the age of 12, I lost my nerve.

I was such a typical boy. I would shy away from girls. Almost absurdly so. One summer holiday when I must have been eight or nine a gang of us, both boys and girls, were messing about on the slides and swings on the green. It felt like we'd been there all day. And then one of the girls suggested some silly game of dressing up, an innocent charade. And a couple of the lads joined in with gusto, reappearing from the girl's house in her clothes – her brownie uniform, that sort of thing. Just funny dressing-up stuff. And we all laughed at the ridiculousness of it all. But I couldn't go. I hung back. I stayed on my own on the swing, probably made a few wisecracks – at least the best an eight-year-old can muster. I wanted to play along, but was too scared. I was stupidly scared of what my gran would say – she used to sit up at that flat window of hers and watch everything, at least that's what I believed. I was scared of being called a sissy by someone, anyone. I was scared that someone would see that I enjoyed it too much and felt too much at home or at ease in girls' clothing.

The crucial thing in all this was that, as uncomfortable as I increasingly became in my body, I still had an awful lot of fun as a boy. This is so hard to admit: that I actually enjoyed being a boy and a young man. There was so much that was good and should not be forgotten and should be celebrated and does not deserve to be lost. It is this that I have often found difficult to embrace. Being male gave me opportunities that I probably would have struggled to get if I had been a natural-born girl. Not only did I get to learn guitar, but I got to really rock and metal out like it was then still only possible to do as a man. The music I grew to love and love still – metal, rock and prog – may well have been the same if I'd been a girl; but I got to do it without apology because they were the kinds of music that, in those days, it was OK for a man to love. I got to be free to dick about and hang out with people in ways I suspect might have been more restricted for a girl. I had so much freedom, so many laughs and so much silliness.

I got to do all the things that are expected from young men and I had a total ball. OK, instinct tells me that one of the reasons I always had to go further than everyone else – whether in drinking or taking drugs or stupid antics (there was a time when I'd do almost anything for a dare) – was because of my basic unhappiness, but the simple fact was that I got to pack more fun into a few years than many do in a lifetime. Even when the drug-taking became rather bleak – I think I spent the whole of 1990 utterly addled on a combination of weed, mushrooms, LSD & speed –

and I was trying to use them to blot things out, I came through. And now I'm glad for the experience.

We all create myths for ourselves. Every time we try to tell our story we do this. For telling our story or giving our point of view requires that we are selective. We pick out this detail, we exclude or ignore that. Our choices of what to include and exclude reveal how we see ourselves and, when it comes to how we share our 'grand' story, how we mythologise ourselves. If someone asks us, 'Who are you?' we can answer in a thousand different ways, but each will reveal something about what we imagine our identity is grounded in. That is, the founding myths of ourselves. As a trans woman, I have often been extraordinarily selective in how I tell my story and, of course, for the sake of getting on with my life, this is entirely reasonable. Anyone with sense will find the right occasions in which to disclose and to be discreet. But I have come to understand the extent to which I have attempted to be discreet around myself and the extent to which I have tried to block from myself not just details but a deep truth: that in so many ways I enjoyed being a man and I got so many goods from it.

This process of what might be called reverse reconciliation has been a long time coming. After the experiments of my twenties, when I guess I tried to be as girly and as womanly as I could, I have found my way back to myself. Consider, for example, the somewhat shallow, but nonetheless important, dimension of dress. Like most grown women, I have reached a point where I know what I like but also know what works for me clothes-wise. And that means avoiding, as much as other women, certain styles of dress. I have come to terms with the fact that my music and cinema taste is – if one were to stereotype – a little more male than that of most women of my age. I do play the boyish image when it comes to expressing my sexuality and am very happy with that. But I have only really just begun to be unafraid of the fact that not only was I such a typical male child, but that that past was genuinely good.

I've sometimes wondered how my life might have been if I had spoken up at an earlier age about my desire to be a girl. From the perspective of comfortable middle age, conscious of the opportunity I missed to be a young woman, I really wish I'd spoken up, even as I know that that desire is based on a high degree of fantasy and wish-fulfilment. For that wish excludes the considerable anxiety, bullying and trouble that would have ensued. Intriguingly, back in about 2002, when I was living in Salford, I had a startling glimpse of what my life might have been like if I had only been more confident, a little braver as a child. I was on a bus in Langworthy, one of the toughest areas in Manchester, and on stepped a mother and daughter. They sat opposite me and I barely gave them a second look. And then I noticed that the girl wasn't a girl, as such, but a young boy, maybe about ten, dressed in a extremely gender neutral way, with a face full of make-up on. He looked really very happy with himself, and his mum was quite unselfconscious. They were off into town. The make-up was maybe a bit over the top (but life can be over the top in Langworthy), but instinct told me that this boy wasn't just playing 'dress up'; or if he was, he just didn't give a damn.

Could that have been me if only I'd have been braver? Probably not. My world was very small and conservative. My world was from another time. I do not think I could have survived the bullying, cruelty and misunderstanding my decision would have generated. Much as I like to imagine that the world has become more understanding of the gender dysphoric, I guess this lad/lass probably had a hard time of it. But I was stupidly jealous and full of admiration for his/her honesty. I wish I could have been like that.

At the same time, I am a divided self. For as much as I might wish I could have been bolder in speaking out sooner about my gender dysphoria, I am conscious of this journey of reconciliation I am on. My childhood was both good and worthwhile; I enjoyed so much of it and got to do so many fun and silly things. My teens were not a write-off and I look back on those times – inevitably with slightly rosy spectacles – as both rewarding and excellent. Because of the choice I made to keep quiet I really got to shine and those days have helped make me who I am. It has taken me many years of honest and authentic self-reflection and living with God to become at peace with the simple unavoidable fact that some aspects of my past life are dissonant with where and who I am now. For me, the immense and joyous good news is that such dissonance, paradox and inconsistency are creative, thrilling and risky in the best sense of the words. The 'shalom' in my Self, which is very real, is not of a comforting and easily resolved kind. It is the creative dissonance of (to borrow a phrase of Gillian Rose) the 'Broken Middle'. In terms of my private life, the notion of the 'Broken Middle' feels true and fruitful. The concept gestures towards the truth that being a trans-woman is never simple and involves, for me at least, negotiating a reality that brings with it traces of being a boy and man as well as being a woman. And broken? Yes, but it would be lazy to assume that I take this word in a negative way. I, like all human beings, am broken. Perhaps I am more broken than most; I do not know. But I know also that my brokenness – which includes some aspects of my gender dysphoria, but is most certainly not defined by it – is also a place of creativity, hope and healing. This creativity is, I sense, an emergent property of forging wholeness out of pain and confusion, but crucially is a reflection of an essential and defining truth of the Christian faith: that it is out of woundedness and brokenness themselves that new life, 'shalom', and creation come. But this no shalom *in stasis* but the shalom in journey and transformation. Surely Christ's wounds, the very wellspring of new hope, teach us precisely that.

There is such a thing as grace. It is what makes it possible for us embrace the broken, to go beyond our places of safety and prejudice and, by reconciling those things which seem impossible, it brings us new hope. I do not care if you choose to see this grace as the work of God or not. It is real. And within it I have begun to find a way to a place where I both rejoice in who I am and what I have become, but also delight in where I have been. I am a woman but for the first time I can begin to say that I am glad that I was a man.

Postscript

I am walking down the main street of Stourport-upon-Severn. There is a stench of fish and chips and fried food on the air. The tawdry lights of the Riverside Amusements, a permanent fun fair next to the Severn, flash and shine. The elegant buildings – erected by ambitious Georgian burghers, awash with canal revenues and hope – have long since been turned into showy shop fronts selling cheap alcohol and second-rate fancy goods. There is a pub on every corner.

Some things never change.

There are people too. A couple of lads on bikes roll past, chip forks speared through the polystyrene cartons holding their tea. A knot of teenagers lolls outside the Flam, Bridge Street's little amusement arcade, giggling and flirting, the oldest girl taking a drag on a rat-faced boy's fag. The fine art of teenage seduction. And there is what passes for a post-work crowd in these parts: two or three besuited individuals, heads aimed at the ground, hurrying home, as if worried the street will swallow them whole.

This is a town to escape from. A one-street town. A dormitory town for those who spend most of their waking lives elsewhere: in Birmingham, Worcester or, God spare us, Redditch. This has always been a town to escape from. And my first plan – as a fifteen-year-old beginning to think about what adulthood might look like – was always to escape. Those of us at school with a bit of nous and brain made sure we did. Yes, we returned for annual drinking binges, and university holidays, and friends' weddings and parties, but we made sure we got away.

Perhaps there is never really any escape for any of us from the places where we grew up, especially if we lived in one settled location. No matter how shabby, how disappointing, how uninspiring, it always remains in one sense 'home'. The older we get, the less we can escape our youth. And perhaps that's the real price I pay for the choices I've made. The further I walk away from my childhood, my teens and my male youth, the clearer it becomes that, no matter how much I am at ease with myself, no matter how right the decisions I have made, there is a huge part of me that is lost and can never be found.

Perhaps that is simply how it is for all of us. The tantalising dream is that, somehow, if only we are committed or energetic or caring enough, there is a way in which the disparate threads of our lives can be woven together. In which our childhood and adulthood might be made one. And yet I sense – because of my radical decisions – I feel it more keenly. From time to time I make genuine efforts to connect up with old friends from my youth and exchange mails or meet up and it's fun or awkward or interesting, depending upon the person. Then we part and move on and forget each other again. As we should. For we have our own separate lives now and a shared, distant past is not enough to hold us.

My longing for a lost youth – a simple youth of weekends spent down by the river messing around with friends, talking music and girls, dreaming of escape and being rock stars and quoting Monty Python lines at each other – feels childish and simplistic. Yet, compared to the choices I've since made, that time does feel simple. And I do feel regret for what I've done. The natural path my life should have taken was destroyed and with it a whole pattern of friendships and stories.

I read once that the light we see in the night sky is simply the faint echo of a long-dead star. Long since gone, long since dark. And that is how my past often seems to me: a trick of time and space, the light of a dark star, an echo of something already dead. And yet seemingly still alive.

And so finally I know why I am walking towards the river.

I go down the steps at the side of the bridge and across the grassy park towards the water. I see that pair of lads on their bikes racing away along the path, their polystyrene-covered teas carried like treasure in their hands. I see a middle-aged couple walking towards me, hand in hand, the woman smiling at the man.

I see my fifteen-year-old self – spotty, with greasy hair, a long grey trench coat – sat on the swings, earnestly discussing the merits of Marillion over Iron Maiden with a gang of friends.

I see my seventeen-year-old self – leaner, with long curly hair, wearing a Jethro Tull t-shirt – sat on the grass on a summer's day, trying to impress my first proper girlfriend with talk of Sartre and Camus.

I see my twenty-year-old self – with a beard and dreadlocks, twinkling eyes – down in the park late at night, rolling a spliff, regaling old friends with tales of university madness. Laughing his head off as if he were king of the world.

And for a moment our eyes lock – his and mine ... and he nods and smiles ...

And I try to speak, to say something.

But he is already gone.

And the river flows slowly on. And in the distance, two boys on bikes disappear through the trees.

Acknowledgements

Thank you to Nicola Slee, Rosie Miles, Alison Peacock, Jeffrey Wainwright, Alastair Barrett & Hilary and Tom Thomas for reading early drafts. Your comments and generosity brought clarity to my ill-expressed thoughts. Thanks also to *The Church Times*, especially Rachel Boulding, for publishing a short section of chapter nine.

About the Author

Rachel Mann is a parish priest in Manchester, UK. She is Resident Poet at Manchester Cathedral and is a former Teaching Fellow in philosophy at Lancaster University. Her poems, liturgy and essays have been widely published, including several by Wild Goose. She is also a freelance music journalist with interests in metal, prog and folk.

Bibliography

Clearly it would be absurd to suggest that I am the first person who has ever travelled the paths outlined in this book – whether that be in gender, theological or spiritual terms. For the sake of readability I have sought to keep the footnotes to a minimum. Nonetheless, I owe a huge debt not only to writers cited in the text but to countless other scholars and thinkers. This bibliography represents a small sample of influential books. I begin with those I have directly cited and move to those that have influenced my thinking over many years.

Aeschylus, *Oresteia* (Chicago: Chicago University Press, 1953)

Aristotle, *Nicomachean Ethics* (London: Penguin 1970)

Neil Astley (ed.), *Staying Alive: Real Poems for Unreal Times*, (Tarset, Bloodaxe Books, 2002)

John Barton, *Tantalus: An Epic for Our Time* ((London: Oberon Books, 2000)

John Bell & Harold Owen, *Wilfred Owen: Collected Letters* (Oxford: OUP 1967)

Eavan Boland, *Selected Poems* (Manchester: Carcanet 1989)

Barbara Brown Taylor, *When God is Silent* (Boston: Cowley 1998)

John Dower, *War Without Mercy* (London: Faber 1986)

Euripides, *Orestes and Other Plays* (London: Penguin 1972)

Belden C. Lane, *The Solace of Fierce Landscapes: Exploring Desert & Mountain Spirituality* (Oxford: OUP 1998)

Thomas Merton, *Seeds of Contemplation* (London: Hollis & Carter 1956)

Bonnie Miller-McLemore & Brita Gill-Austern, eds, *Feminist and Womanist Pastoral Theology* (Nashville, Abingdon, 1999)

Janet Morley, *All Desires Known* (London: SPCK 1988)

Martha Nussbaum, *The Fragility of Goodness* (Cambridge: CUP 1986)

Adrienne Rich, *The Fact of a Doorframe*, Collected Poems 1950-1984, New York, Norton, 1984.

Gillian Rose, *Love's Work* (London: Chatto & Windus 1995)

Jean-Paul Sartre (trans. Philip Mairet), *Existentialism & Humanism* (London: Methuen 1973)

Elisabeth Schüssler Fiorenza, *In Memory of Her* (London: SCM 1996)
Nicola Slee & Rosie Miles (eds), *Doing December Differently* (Glasgow: Wild Goose Publications 2006)
Nicola Slee, *A Book of Mary* (London: SPCK 2007)
Nicola Slee, *The Public Use of Poetry*, Audenshaw Papers 215, 2005, Hinksey Network
Elizabeth Stuart, *Daring to Speak God's Name* (London, Hamish Hamilton, 1992)
Michael Symmons Roberts, *Corpus* (London: Cape 2006)
Charles Taylor, *A Secular Age* (Cambridge: Belknap 2007)
Henry Vaughan, *The Complete Poems* (London: Penguin 1976)
Marina Warner, *Alone of All Her Sex: The Myth & Cult of the Virgin Mary* (London: Vintage 2000)
Sam Wells, *Transforming Fate into Destiny: The Theological Ethics of Stanley Hauerwas* (Carlisle: Paternoster 1998)
Rowan Williams, *Headwaters* (Oxford: Perpetua 2008)

Selected further reading
James Alison, *Undergoing God* (London: DLT 2006)
Mary Ann Beavis (ed), *The Lost Coin: Parables of Women, Work & Wisdom* (Sheffield: Sheffield Academic Press 2002)
Dietrich Bonhoeffer, *Letters and Papers from Prison* (London: SCM 1953)
Judith Butler, *Gender Trouble* (New Ed) (London: Routledge 2006)
René Girard, *Violence and the Sacred* (Baltimore: John Hopkins UP, 1972)
Robert E Goss, *Queering Christ: Beyond Jesus Acted Up* (Resource Publications 2006)
Thomas H. Green, *When the Well Runs Dry* (Notre Dame: Ave Maria Press 1998)
Michael Kirwan, *Discovering Girard* (London: DLT 2004)
Jeffrey Kripal, *Roads of Excess, Palaces of Wisdom: Eroticism & Reflexivity in the Study of Mysticism* (Chicago: University of Chicago Press 2001)
Rosemary Radford Reuther (ed), *Feminist Theologies: Legacy & Prospect* (Minneapolis: Fortress 2007)

Nicola Slee, *Women's Faith Development: Patterns and Processes* (Aldershot: Ashgate 2004)

Nicola Slee, *Praying Like a Woman* (London: SPCK 2004)

Elizabeth Stuart, *Just Good Friends – Towards a Lesbian & Gay Theology of Relationships* (London: Mowbray 1995)

Phyllis Trible, *God and the Rhetoric of Sexuality* (Philadelphia: Fortress 1978)

Phyllis Trible, *Texts of Terror – Feminist Readings of Biblical Narratives* (Philadelphia: Fortress 1984)

Marcella Althaus-Reid, *From Feminist Theology to Indecent Theology* (London: SCM 2004)

Michel Foucault (trans. Alan Sheridan), *Discipline and Punish* (London: Penguin 1991)

Michel Foucault (trans. Robert Hurley), *The History of Sexuality* vols 1-3 (London: Penguin 1990)

Kate Bornstein, *Gender Outlaw – On Men, Women and the Rest of Us* (London: Routledge 2004)

Ludwig Wittgenstein, *On Certainty* (Oxford: Blackwell 1984)

Frank Wright, *The Pastoral Nature of the Ministry* (London: SCM 1980)

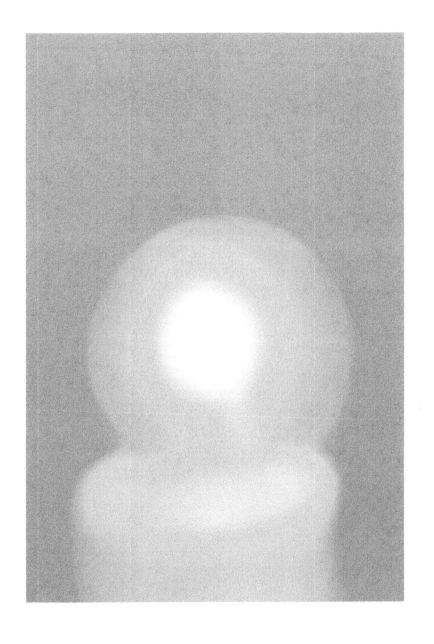

Wild Goose Publications is part of the Iona Community:

- An ecumenical movement of men and women from different walks of life and different traditions in the Christian church
- Committed to the gospel of Jesus Christ, and to following where that leads, even into the unknown
- Engaged together, and with people of goodwill across the world, in acting, reflecting and praying for justice, peace and the integrity of creation
- Convinced that the inclusive community we seek must be embodied in the community we practise

Together with our staff, we are responsible for:
- Our islands residential centres of Iona Abbey, the MacLeod Centre on Iona, and Camas Adventure Centre on the Ross of Mull

and in Glasgow:
- The administration of the Community
- Our work with young people
- Our publishing house, Wild Goose Publications
- Our association in the revitalising of worship with the Wild Goose Resource Group

The Iona Community was founded in Glasgow in 1938 by George MacLeod, minister, visionary and prophetic witness for peace, in the context of the poverty and despair of the Depression. Its original task of rebuilding the monastic ruins of Iona Abbey became a sign of hopeful rebuilding of community in Scotland and beyond. Today, we are about 280 members, mostly in Britain, and about 1500 associate members, with over 1400 friends worldwide. Together and apart, 'we follow the light we have, and pray for more light'.

For information on the Iona Community contact:
The Iona Community, 21 Carlton Court, Glasgow G5 9JP, UK.
Phone: 0141 429 7281
e-mail: admin@iona.org.uk; web: www.iona.org.uk

For enquiries about visiting Iona, please contact:
Iona Abbey, Isle of Iona, Argyll PA76 6SN, UK. Phone: 01681 700404
e-mail: ionacomm@iona.org.uk